More Praise for *The L*

"Simple, memorable, and powerful, T
any organization embrace their humanity in ways that improve
performance both inside and out. We could all stand to have a little
more LUCK in our lives."

- Jeff Rohrs, Author, *Audience*

"Ables has tackled one of the biggest challenges facing businesses
this century - keeping people at the center of an increasingly digital
world - and delivered the answers that executives are searching for."

- Michael Gentle, Author, The CRM Project Management
Handbook, and co-founder, Fly Another Day

"Finally, an intelligent treatment of business relationships. It's not
about delivering doughnuts or some vague, touchy/feely "thing"
that we must all do well. Establishing and nurturing relationships
is a process that can (and must!) be measured, and thereby continuously improved. Geoff nailed it."

- Todd Youngblood, Author, *Think About It...*

"While digital technology has the potential to bring internal teams
and customers together, few organizations have successfully tran-
sitioned a 1:1 mentality into the digital age. The LUCK Principle
provides a clear roadmap for leveraging big data, analytics, digital
channels and a strong culture to create more engaged employees
and a better customer experience. Beyond being a book for better
relationships in business, it is a book for better relationships in life."

- Jim Marous, Owner of the Digital Banking Report,
Co-Publisher of The Financial Brand

"The LUCK Principle contains new insight into timeless truths about relationships in business, and in life. Ables delivers this in the format of an incredibly useful story that anyone can relate to, and organized into an understandable process."

- Stephen Montague, President and COO, Midrex Technologies

"The LUCK Principle is about the people side of business, a creative roadmap focusing on why human relationships are critical to the success of an enterprise. It ties together the needs and motivations of both employees and customers in dynamic feedback loops that fuel innovation as a company scales. Empathy and data are shown to work seamlessly together in an environment of openness, awareness, and constant improvement."

- Ken Goldstein, Author, *Endless Encores* and *This Is Rage*

"Business is about people. This book will transform your people strategy. Buy it, apply it, and pass it on to your CMO, CIO and HR Director."

- Chris Elmore, Author, *The Argument to Automate*

"Everything in business and in life starts and ends with people. The LUCK Principle brings this to life through a story that is as inspiring as it is actionable. Whether for business or private life, LUCK is all you need."

- Denyse Drummond-Dunn, Author,
Winning Customer Centricity

THE LUCK PRINCIPLE^(TM)

THE LUCK PRINCIPLE(TM)

BUSINESS RESULTS AT THE INTERSECTION OF PEOPLE AND PROFIT

Geoff Ables

ISBN-13: 9780997680300
ISBN-10: 099768030X
Library of Congress Control Number: 2016909899
Wilmington Publishing, Charlotte, North Carolina

Contents

Every business exists to serve people. Serving a large number of customers and employees in today's digital world is a complex endeavor, and as a result, most books on the subject are complex and technical. This book takes a different approach. Read this section to get a fast overview.

#DigitalWorkplace #HumanTouch

When organizations engage employees and customers, they achieve breakthrough performance. Businesses invest billions in pursuit of such results, but the outcomes have mostly been disappointing. Legacy approaches to solving business problems no longer work. The convergence of the digital and human worlds requires a new way of thinking about relationships. LUCK is a framework of timeless principles that the best relationship builders have used for thousands of years, scaled to work in a complex business environment.

#BigData #OmniChannel

Rapidly expanding communication channels are creating data-rich, communication-poor businesses. Discover why this is destroying employee performance, job satisfaction, and the customer's experience. See what you can do to transform how your organization listens to the voices of customers and employees.

#Analytics #Insights

Transforming data gathered through listening into actionable insights is the job of every person in the organization—not just that of a few analysts and executives. Every organization has the most important data it needs, yet few make it easy for employees to find it. Learn why almost every business gets distracted by "big data" and discover strategies for converting data into insights and insights into action.

#CustomerExperience #Process

When it comes to relationships, connecting is where the action is—but the action is not what most people think it is. Debunk the myth that good relationships involve more art than science. Learn why process is the key to creating connections and how relationship processes are different from traditional business processes. Discover how to manage good connections, bad connections, weak ties, and strong ties to better deliver agility and innovation.

#Collaboration #Innovation

Organizations where employees know the score, can measure their contribution, and are invited to participate in improving and innovating don't just win the game—they change the game. Learn the role of metrics, failure, meetings, and vulnerability in creating a culture of constant improvement and innovation.

#Leadership #Balance

Combine bottom-line focus with a people-first philosophy, a critical balance for success in the twenty-first century. Learn how to adjust these two typically conflicting priorities to sustain employee engagement, customer satisfaction, and business returns. Understand why creating a sustained commitment to delivering great customer experiences goes beyond projects, technology tools, and mission statements.

Apply sound relationship principles as a strategy for transforming a business, making it a continuous effort. The LUCK Principle can be applied to every area of business and life—with both improving as a result.

Join the community, explore additional resources, learn to apply the LUCK Principle to everything, and have a little fun along the way.

ABOUT THIS BOOK

What is our business? Who is our customer?
What does the customer consider value?
—PETER DRUCKER

The more technologically advanced our society
becomes, the more we need to go back to the basic
fundamentals of human communication.
—ANGELA AHRENDTS

Never forget that absolutely everything
you do is for your customers.
—DEREK SIVERS

Life in business isn't always about calculators and
dollars...the relationships have to be right.
—MARCUS LEMONIS

Warning: This Book Is Dangerous
—JON STONE

The forces of massive data, advanced analytical and machine learning tools, consumer-driven communication channels, mobile technology, the Internet of things, and for the first time in history, a workforce that spans five generations have reshaped the world of business. At the center of this change is the person, the desire to deliver a better relationship experience to the customer and employee, and the technology to transform the desire into reality at a large scale.

Relationships make up the raw material for organizational success. Technology, process, and analytical capabilities to support relationships are fast transitioning from a competitive advantage to a requirement for survival.

This book deals with relationships.

It's about personal relationships and the simple principles world-class relationship builders have practiced for thousands of years. The book explores business relationships and how they can successfully scale those simple relationship practices to work in a complex business setting.

Over the past twenty years, companies have invested billions in improving how they engage employees and manage customer relationships. Research suggests that relationships remain one of the few remaining areas for competitive differentiation in business, and as a result, the forecast predicts very high investment in this area for the foreseeable future. In spite of all this investment, studies regularly report abysmal failure rates of 30 to 60 percent for these initiatives, and nearly half of organizations fail two or more times before getting it right or giving up. There exists a chasm of failure between the status quo and the promised land of engaged customers and employees.

The good news? Transforming how your business engages people doesn't require a revolution (revolutions, after all, are often bloody and destructive). Instead, a well-planned set of evolutionary steps, The LUCK Principle, can deliver the sought-after results.

This book, based on years of research and experience with customer and employee engagement, simplifies the challenge of business relationships by drawing a parallel between successful individual relationships and the methods by which they can be scaled to work in large, complex businesses. This investigation is presented in quickly digestible story, infographic, and case-study formats. The field trips in each chapter comprise a cross-section of real-life case studies shared in interviews and client engagements. Each chapter concludes with a journal entry and application section to aid you in applying the lessons found to your own situation.

In the course of the book, you will be introduced to Lauren, the owner of a small-town coffee shop, and the five timeless principles of Good LUCK that she has applied to her life. You will also meet her son, Patrick, as he reflects back on lessons learned in the coffee shop and scales the principles to work in a corporate environment.

You may find this book challenging to your ideas regarding the purpose of business and nature of interpersonal relationships. It may challenge you to give up control in some areas and seize more control in others. The principles and values contained in the book, however, are based on proven patterns that lead to success, both personally and on a corporate level. Those who accept the challenge will find themselves on a sometimes difficult but ultimately rewarding journey.

You will find that the concepts behind LUCK are simple—even obvious. Sometimes the most obvious thing is the most revolutionary one. But as you begin to put these concepts into practice, you will find that though they are simple, they are not easy.

The LUCK Principle can be applied to any way we relate to one another or even to ourselves. While the primary focus of the book is on how to scale The LUCK Principle to work in a corporate environment, the principles work in every environment in which relationships are important: individual relationships, project management, running meetings, and more importantly, a relationship with yourself.

Good luck on your journey into Good LUCK!

Learn More

Register your copy of the book at www.theLUCKprinciple.com. As a registered reader of the book, you are entitled to download the accompanying e-book containing more detailed infographics and insights. You can also sign up for the blog to continue to receive the latest information on improving the customer experience, employee engagement, and business profits.

ACKNOWLEDGMENTS

STOP.

E veryone skips the acknowledgments, except for people who know the author. But this is a book about relationships, and it is a book written because of relationships. Understanding the acknowledgments is part of understanding this book. I encourage you, reader, to take a few moments to read through this section before proceeding.

Writing the acknowledgments surprised me—it was the most challenging part of this book to write. In fact, it almost didn't make the final cut. The relationships, research, and writing that went into this book spans over ten years and comes from hundreds of clients, colleagues, friends, and family members sharing their stories and lessons. There are far too many to name, so I won't. But here is an idea of who they are and what they contributed:

- Partners—in business and in life—who encouraged me to write the book and who cheerfully carried the weight of running a business and a household while I was writing.

- Leaders and mentors who are a part of Young Life. The people of Young Life give so much to so many, and live out the heart of LUCK every day. You are my coffee shop experience.

- The owners and regulars at In the Wind Bar and Grill. They provided a stool to sit on and a table for my laptop. Strangers there became friends and freely shared their stories, inspiration, and insights. If you're ever in Huntersville, North Carolina, stop by for a beer and a burger and meet the bikers who hang out there.

- Clients and those who have listened to my talks on LUCK. Trying to serve them is, ultimately, the source of The LUCK Principle. Listening to them over many years has fine-tuned the concepts behind LUCK.

- Authors who had nothing to gain by helping, but who nonetheless graciously and freely shared their time, insights, and connections to help make this book better.

- Friends, family, business contacts, and near-strangers who provided feedback and even a place to stay when I needed a quiet place to work.

Here is what we can all learn about LUCK from these individuals:

People are amazing. They will surprise you with their generosity if you let them. Although there are always those who will turn away or even stand in the way, there are also many who want to help. When you let them become a part of your journey, you are serving them on their journeys, as well.

In today's fast-moving and complex world, we need to work together better than ever before, if we are to meet the challenges that we face in business and society. We need to learn how to draw a bigger circle and invite others in. We need to learn how to some-times accept the invitation to join others in the circles that they are drawing.

Thank you to the hundreds who have contributed to this project and who have shared this lesson with all who will read this book.

Introduction

If you want to go fast, go alone. If you
want to go far, go with others.
—African Proverb

I am a great believer in luck, and I find the
harder I work, the more I have of it.
—Thomas Jefferson

Scaling is about spreading a mindset,
not just a footprint.
—Robert Sutton

I don't know where we should take this company, but
I do know that if I start with the right people, ask
them the right questions, and engage them in vigorous
debate, we will find a way to make this company great.
—Jim Collins

A cardinal principle of Total Quality
escapes too many managers; you cannot
continuously improve interdependent systems

and processes until you progressively perfect
interdependent, interpersonal relationships.
—STEPHEN COVEY

CEO.

He had known for a while that he would be considered for the position when the time came.

Patrick had joined the successful, growing company, straight out of college. The relatively small team had an exceptional ability to work together and showed passion about serving customers. As the small team grew, however, it lost something. Employee satisfaction dipped, customer loyalty faltered, and business growth plateaued. Technology didn't solve the problem and in some cases made it worse. But Patrick steadily applied his family's LUCK Principle, and as a result, the situation turned around before it became dire.

"I recommended, and the board has agreed, that you should be my replacement," the retiring CEO said. She continued, "Not because of the growth in profits, market share, and employee satisfaction you've contributed to. But because you have forever changed the way we work together with one another and with our customers. You've changed how we think as a business. You've taken that thinking and you've found ways to harness technology to scale how we manage relationships and collaborate. In other words, you've changed our culture—this is a different place to work than it was when you first arrived here. Even if I fired you, instead of promoting you to CEO, the organization would continue to become more effective because of the way you have invested yourself into it." It was high praise coming from an outgoing CEO, one with a tough reputation and a fierce temper, which had sometimes been directed at Patrick.

The reality that the promotion would be announced in one week began to sink in. Patrick had taken the week off to relax and reenergize before stepping into the new role. Besides, it was Patrick's annual tradition to visit his family back home in their small seaside town in eastern North Carolina for the annual Saint Paddy's Day festival, so the timing was perfect.

He could walk to the park in the town square from his childhood home and where he still stayed when he came to town. The park played host to most of the festival. Organizers set up a fairground, and a parade that lasted only about an hour would go down the street between the park and his mother's coffee shop. His mother, Lauren, had founded the coffee shop, The Lion's Den, with Aunt Mallorie, a few years before Patrick had been born.

Everyone else had left earlier that morning to help his mother open the coffee shop, as she had been doing just about every morning of Patrick's life. He told them he had to check some email, but had really stayed behind to have a little bit of time to reflect and plan.

Although the promotion hadn't surprised him, he was still more than a little anxious about the new role. How could a quiet, introverted, small-town kid eventually become the head of a company with thousands of employees, millions of customers, and operations on five continents? Would the same things that took him from an engineering degree to the research and development department, to customer service, and most recently to vice president of sales, marketing, and service be the same things the company required from its CEO to continue growing and engaging its employees and customers?

Patrick left the house and started the walk toward The Lion's Den with these things still on his mind.

"Happy Saint YOU Day, Patrick, me friend!" The booming voice shook Patrick out of his thoughts. Even with the phony Irish accent, he instantly recognized the voice of his old high-school buddy, Chris, and the "Saint YOU Day" joke he had been using ever since they had met. Chris had become the figurehead of the St. Patrick's Day celebration in the town. He was dressed in green from his top hat to his pointy shoes, and Patrick couldn't help but to break into a wide grin at the sight of him.

"Yer clearly lost in thought, Patrick. What's on yer mind?" Chris inquired, still with the comical attempt at an accent.

Patrick relayed the news of the promotion and his concerns about his readiness for such an enormous job.

"Ah see. Then you'll be needin' this more than I will, me friend." Chris handed Patrick a card, then hurried away to go tend to getting the parade started.

Patrick resumed his walk and soon found himself just a few doors away from The Lion's Den. He looked at the card. It was square and slightly smaller than a playing card. On it was the word "Good" in green, and below this was a four leaf clover, each leaf having one letter of the word "LUCK" printed on it. "Good LUCK."

Patrick's mind was immediately transported to almost the exact spot he stood now about thirty years earlier.

Infographic

Customer and employee
ENGAGEMENT
have a transformational impact on business...

When organizations successfully engage their customers and employees, they experience a 240% boost in performance-related business outcomes compared with an organization with neither engaged employees nor engaged customers.[1]

The average payback on every dollar spent on relationship management and collaboration projects.[2]

But success is elusive.

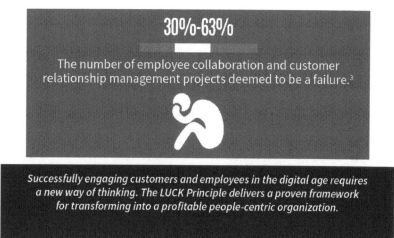

30%-63%

The number of employee collaboration and customer relationship management projects deemed to be a failure.[3]

Successfully engaging customers and employees in the digital age requires a new way of thinking. The LUCK Principle delivers a proven framework for transforming into a profitable people-centric organization.

Download the full Infographic at: www.theLUCKprinciple.com/gotBook

In The Lion's Den

During his senior year of high school, Patrick slogged through the college admissions process, and things weren't going well. He had applied for early admissions to several state schools with engineering programs, and none had accepted him. Now he pushed through the standard admissions process. For over a year, his mother had been encouraging him to set up meetings with admissions officers, professors, and anyone else who would meet with Patrick, and he decided the situation finally warranted such tactics. It was the eve of his first visit to a campus, and Patrick was anxious.

Patrick helped his mother shut down The Lion's Den at the end of the day, as he often did. A few customers lingered, sipping coffee, beer, or nibbling on homemade cookies. Patrick took twice as long to do everything as he normally did, as he tried to think of things he should say in the admissions meeting the next day.

"Patrick, sweetie, your head's in the clouds. What's the matter, honey?" Patrick's mother, Lauren, spoke in a soft Southern accent. She always spoke slowly and clearly, as if inviting the listener to speak. Lauren had grown up in the small town of Mansura, Louisiana, and her family had lived there for many generations. She first came to North Carolina to attend college but created quite a stir when she announced that she would be marrying her college boyfriend before graduation and would be staying in North Carolina. It created an even bigger stir when her younger sister, Mallorie, announced three years later that she too would move to North Carolina to purchase an old coffee shop with Lauren and go into business with her.

The coffee shop business had steadily blossomed into an art center, weekend music hall and pub, college hangout in the winter, and tourist attraction in the summer. The town square in which the coffee shop was located had been there since shortly after the town had been founded over 150 years earlier. The hardwood floors of the shop harkened back to the classic oceanfront designs popular when the community had first become a vacation destination shortly after the Second World War—the last time the shop had been remodeled. The worn counter that ran almost the full length of the shop bore the nicks and scratches of thousands of mugs of coffee that had passed across it. The coffee machines were the latest available models, but they were well hidden behind the counter so that they didn't interfere with the otherwise time-worn feel of the place. The shop felt as if it had been made more inviting and somehow, wiser, by the salty ocean air. It was a place full of memories and lessons learned for Patrick.

"You know I'm going to meet with two people for college admissions tomorrow. I've no idea what to say to impress them." Patrick had picked up his mother's quiet but confident and engaging cadence when speaking, although her lilting Southern accent had not been transferred to Patrick.

"Don't worry about saying the right thing, just rely on a lot of luck."

There was a moment of silence.

"C'mon, Mom!" Patrick exclaimed, "You know getting into a good engineering school is important to me. I know you don't believe in luck. How on earth is that supposed to help me?"

"Sugar, I don't mean 'luck,' I mean 'L-U-C-K,' in capitals," she said, spelling out the word. "Come sit down." Patrick sat down at the long and well-worn wooden coffee bar, and his mother stood on the other side and talked while she continued to work.

"Patrick, the truth is there's nothing you can tell those folks that they haven't already seen on your application and that they haven't already heard from a thousand other kids like you," Lauren started. "But you can *listen* to them. So few people are good listeners—especially people your age. As you listen to them, you will begin to *understand* them and their school. People want to know they are understood. When you understand them, then you can *connect* with them—talking about the things that are of interest to both you and them. It takes some practice, but you'll *know* how you're doing by how they respond to you.

"Do you get my meaning now, honey? LUCK stands for listen, understand, connect, and know. Your great-grandfather taught that to me, and it has been the one thing that has helped me most in building better relationships with people throughout my life. He said it helped him to develop lasting relationships with customers when he sold shoes after he came to America. Everybody uses LUCK every day to build relationships, but very few people do it well and consistently. I've learned The LUCK Principle is as timeless as it is simple—it has worked for me for over thirty years while engaging with friends, customers, and employees—it worked for your great-grandfather pretty well, too."

"The Good Book says, 'Do unto others as you would have them do unto you,' and LUCK just helps your mother and I put that into practice," Aunt Mallorie said. She had been listening to the conversation. She possessed a different personality from Patrick's mother. She had created or selected most of the art on the walls and had some art on her body, as well, including a large tattoo on one of her arms, one on the opposite wrist, and a third one about the size of a Mardi Gras doubloon in the middle of her back. She surfed on a regular basis, ran a small farm behind her house where she raised chickens (and often served them for dinner), was known to smoke a pipe, and had a salty mouth and a fiery temper. Her reputation had earned her the nickname, "Mal," and Patrick had grown up calling her Aunt Mal. At the same time, she frequently quoted "the Good Book," as she called it, taught surfing camp in the summer, and provided her home for use as a shelter for children from abusive families on a regular basis. She was also Patrick's favorite person in the world—you just didn't get any more authentic than Aunt Mal.

"I can see that look in your eyes," continued Aunt Mal. "You're thinking, 'This is just some old-fashioned advice from my mother, it's too simple, and isn't relevant anymore.' You've started to tune her out! I see you."

Patrick started to object, but one glance from Aunt Mal told him that she had his number. The truth was that this was exactly what Patrick had been thinking, and Aunt Mal had an uncanny way of reading him. What she didn't know, however, was that as soon as she had endorsed LUCK, it gave him a whole new perspective. Although Patrick knew his mother was almost always right, he was more inclined to push back on her than on his street-smart Aunt Mal. If she said something was true, it was instantly credible as far as he was concerned.

"Show him Lauren, show him," said Aunt Mal.

Patrick's mother hesitated. It wasn't her style to be so forceful with Patrick. But after a moment, she reached into a drawer behind the counter where she was standing and pulled out a book. Really, it looked more like an old personal journal. It had a soft and weathered leather cover, was clearly quite old, and from where he sat, Patrick could see five section dividers in the book, though he couldn't make out what they said.

"Patrick, what your Aunt Mal is talking about is—"

"What I'm talking about is your mother's Good LUCK journal, Patrick." Aunt Mal cut Lauren off. "The wisdom she has gathered over thirty years and that has made this place, this town, and your family what it is today. Do you realize how extraordinary your situation is, Patrick? It wasn't by accident. It was a lot of work, but also a whole lot of LUCK. He needs to know, Lauren. Tell him."

Lauren paused and looked directly at Aunt Mal. "Would you like to keep telling him, or may I?"

"I hear ya, I hear ya," Aunt Mal grumbled. She grabbed a bottle of local microbrew from behind the bar, opened it, and settled into a nearby chair, careful to put a few chairs between her and Patrick so as not to seem like she was butting in.

"I started this journal while I was still in college," began Lauren. "Right after your grandfather Conrad told me about LUCK." She quickly flipped through the journal. Patrick could see the five dividers had been attached into the journal by hand, and they were titled "Listen," "Understand," "Connect," "Know," and "Good LUCK." The last one looked different from the others—less worn and with fewer pages—as if it had been added some time after the first four. As his mother flipped through the journal, he could see hundreds of handwritten notes. Some of them looked like quotes or references from books, some were diagrams, and others just looked like personal notes. "I've found everything about relationships with people fits into this framework. And as I learn more, I jot down notes to help me remember. Sometimes I learn something from a book or a mentor. Other times it's just a life experience. What I have found is that the harder I work on putting L-U-C-K into practice, the more luck I have.

"LUCK is how your Aunt Mal and I transformed this place from a broken-down coffee shop into a successful business. It's how we expanded to do so many other things, not just with The Lion's Den but also for the people in our community and for the family. There's not enough time to try to explain everything to you now, but let me try to give you a few things to help you with your college goals.

"Tomorrow you'll be meeting with an admissions officer and a professor at one of your top-choice colleges. Start listening to them tonight." She was looking at the journal and fiddling with the "Listen" tab with her thumb. "Learn everything you can about the university and the individuals who are interviewing you. If you have friends going there, contact them. Read every bit of information you can about the school. Write a list of questions you'd like to get answers to or that you think the people you're speaking with will enjoy talking about. When you get to the office, look around at the pictures and books on the shelves and ask about those too. Absorb every bit of information you can. When they answer questions, ask more questions to learn more about their answers—especially when they get excited about what they're saying. Make it your goal to know things about them they might not even remember themselves. That's listening."

"So I impress them with my knowledge of them and the school," Patrick interrupted. He had an analytical mind and this idea of listening appealed to him.

"Not exactly, sweetie," Lauren said. Patrick knew that this was his mother's gentle way of saying, "You're pretty much totally wrong!" He had grown so accustomed to this phrase and the way his mother said it—with a twinkle in her clear blue eyes and not a hint of judgment—that he had been conditioned to stop talking, recognize he was on the wrong track, and give his mother his full attention. She continued, "You're not listening to get what you want. Your goal is to listen because you're sincerely interested. You're listening to understand—not necessarily to respond. Which is the next part." Her thumb moved down to the "Understand" tab. "When you're listening to understand, you want to know what it is they are trying to tell you so well that you may be able to say it back to them better than they can say it themselves. Sometimes it may even mean discovering some things about the individual that they don't even know about themselves yet!"

"Oh, so once I understand what they want, then I explain why I can be the person to give them that," Patrick interrupted again. He heard Aunt Mal heave a sigh and felt her frustrated gaze on him. Lauren reached across the bar and put her small hand over his much larger hand, giving it a gentle squeeze.

"Again, not exactly," she said. "What if what you have to offer isn't a match for what they are looking for? If you're going to build an authentic relationship, you need to keep focused on serving the other person. People can tell when you're not sincere in your interest or in your claims about yourself. More importantly, *you* can tell, and it will change you into a person you don't want to be. Be very careful to remain real."

She went on, moving her thumb down to the "Connect" tab. "When you understand the person, you'll be able to connect with them. This is your chance to talk. To talk about the things they want to know more about. Talk about things that you have in common with them. Sometimes just being that rare person who truly listens to them is all you need to be. Most of the time, though, an initial meeting is the beginning of a long relationship in which you can earn trust. With college, as with so many other relationships, you may learn some things about yourself that'll require hard work before you can move forward."

"Hang on, Mom," Patrick started with some anxiety in his voice. "I want to do everything I can to get into one of these schools. But you're telling me that I don't have a chance of making much impact in one meeting, and there might not be anything I can say to get in."

"That's the reality, honey. The conversation to get into college is a long one. It starts with your grades and activities. Then it extends into relationships with the admissions folks, which may take a while to build—that's why I encouraged you to start meeting with them last year. If everything is very close, then your conversation tomorrow may be just what it takes to get you in. If not, then it may take longer to get where you want to go.

"This is the last step of LUCK." This time she pointed to the "Know" tab. "You'll know if you're successfully working together with the other person after a time, and you can learn and adjust, always improving how you connect with them. Whenever you're building a relationship or trying to accomplish something great— like getting into college—you need to expect to fail a few times, and failure is your best teacher. Learning from failure is the heart of knowing.

"Your best bet for success is that simple—listen, understand, connect, and know." As she said the words, her thumb slid through the first four tabs of the journal again.

There were a few moments of silence. This wasn't the answer Patrick had wanted to hear. As he processed what he had learned, he started to form another question. There must be a faster way to do this, a shortcut that he could try.

Before he could ask the question, Aunt Mal jumped back in. "It's not what you'll hear works out there." She pointed to the front door of the shop. "If all you care about is getting what you want right away or finding a shortcut, then don't use LUCK. If LUCK is going to work, your horizon needs to be much farther than the next conversation—you'll need to be thinking about the lifetime of the relationship, maybe longer."

Patrick wasn't sure if he should smile or grimace. His mother had always taught him with such patience and wisdom, but she always expected him to be independent and to make his own decisions, so she didn't push unless Patrick asked. Aunt Mal, however, always seemed to understand exactly what was going on in Patrick's head. She never hesitated to dive right into his thoughts and lay them all out there for everyone to see. It dawned on Patrick how fortunate he was to have both of them. Rather than giving Aunt Mal more ammunition, he changed the subject.

"What about the last tab? The one labeled 'Good LUCK'?" asked Patrick.

An odd expression crossed Patrick's mother's face. He hadn't seen it before, and there seemed to be some sadness in it. "That's the chapter Gran'Pa Conrad didn't know to teach me about, Patrick," she said, her voice suddenly distant. "I've made a lot of mistakes, and I've had to learn from them. This chapter reminds me that LUCK is something that we also have to apply to ourselves. It has to come from a sincere and authentic place and not be manipulative. Life is a mixture of serving other people while also harnessing energy to pursue our own plans. Sometimes we err too much to one side or the other. To really make LUCK work, you have to make sure you're practicing Good LUCK."

Patrick's mother didn't get emotional often, and when she did, it made Patrick uncomfortable. So he let the subject drop.

"By the time I graduated college," Patrick's mother drew a deep breath, "I knew I wanted to practice The LUCK Principle everywhere. Not just with family and friends but in business too. That's one of the reasons why I started this coffee shop—so I wouldn't lose that intimacy with people that big companies can't sustain. And that's one of the reasons why I've resisted growing too much and instead have helped others to start businesses."

Lauren tucked the book back away in the drawer and pulled out another book from the same drawer. This one was different. It was newer, the design on the leather cover different, and looked unused. "I have a gift I've been waiting for just the right time to give you," Lauren said with an uncertain smile. "This is your LUCK journal, Patrick. Fill it with your own thoughts and lessons learned about how to give yourself and the people around you the gift of LUCK. Add to it, just like I added to what your Gran'Pa Conrad taught me."

Patrick knew his mother had made the journal by hand. In addition to running the coffee shop and having a good business mind, she was also an accomplished artist and had a love of writing, leatherworking, and photography. He also knew all of her commitments had left little time for her to do these things. Gifts such as this one were precious things into which she poured her soul. Patrick hugged his mother without saying a word and resumed his work helping to shut down the shop for the evening—now with more haste so he could get home and start listening.

That day started a change in Patrick.

His plans for college didn't go the way he wanted, and that may have been the best thing that ever happened to him. Although he had good conversations with each of the admissions officers, none of the schools accepted him. So Patrick went to the local community college for the next two years while he continued to work at The Lion's Den. Those two years at the old coffee shop had a profound impact—transforming Patrick's vision of himself from that of a technical wizard engineer into someone who recognized that everything in life, including business, was about relationships. This change in his thinking was subtle in those early years, but it pointed his life in an entirely new direction.

At one point during those two years, Patrick made a decision that he recorded in his own LUCK journal. He had always wanted to work for a company that delivered innovative products to a large number of customers, but like his mother, he didn't want to be a part of something that lost the ability to practice LUCK with the people it served. He would make a project out of scaling LUCK to work in organizations where hundreds or even thousands of employees had to engage with one another, businesses with potentially millions of customers. What he didn't know was that the project would last the rest of his lifetime and present many obstacles and frustrating failures before he unlocked the secrets of scaling LUCK.

Patrick practiced LUCK with the contacts he had made at universities, and after two years at the local community college, he got into his first-choice school. As he launched his career, he found The LUCK Principle was every bit as timeless as his mother had told him. He applied it to every relationship. Taking it further, he shared it with his colleagues and built a track record of high-performance teams. He also began the hard work of scaling it—transforming the principles proven to work in one-on-one relationships to work in complex business relationships with hundreds, thousands, or hundreds of thousands, of employees and customers. Eventually, he found that even newly emerging ways to engage on a massive scale with customers and colleagues neatly fit into the LUCK framework.

His journey to scale LUCK proved far more challenging than he had ever imagined. At every turn, he had to learn the lessons of many failures before finding success. The toughest part of the process, he realized, wasn't technology or even changing how people in a business work together. It was leadership. It took years to get the entire leadership team to embrace a new way of thinking—and to learn how to lead the business using new processes, tools, and metrics. The real transformation began only once the leadership team was aligned.

Now, thirty years after that first conversation about Good LUCK, Patrick stood outside of the shop, still staring at the "Good LUCK" card. Lost in thought, he absentmindedly put his hand on the wooden sign just outside the door and traced the grooves of the carved name of the shop, where only the faintest traces of paint remained. He smiled as he realized that the harder he had worked at LUCK; the more luck he had experienced. He felt a surge of confidence that this simple and timeless principle was exactly what was needed to power his company as he continued to reflect on the journey that had brought him to this moment.

Journal Entry

The LUCK Principle

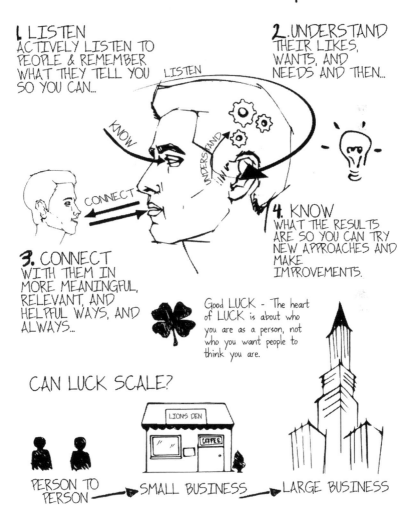

1. LISTEN
ACTIVELY LISTEN TO PEOPLE & REMEMBER WHAT THEY TELL YOU SO YOU CAN...

LISTEN

2. UNDERSTAND
THEIR LIKES, WANTS, AND NEEDS AND THEN...

KNOW

UNDERSTAND

CONNECT

4. KNOW
WHAT THE RESULTS ARE SO YOU CAN TRY NEW APPROACHES AND MAKE IMPROVEMENTS.

3. CONNECT
WITH THEM IN MORE MEANINGFUL, RELEVANT, AND HELPFUL WAYS, AND ALWAYS...

Good LUCK - The heart of LUCK is about who you are as a person, not who you want people to think you are.

CAN LUCK SCALE?

LIONS DEN

COFFEE

PERSON TO PERSON → SMALL BUSINESS → LARGE BUSINESS

19

CHAPTER 1
LISTEN

You can have data without information, but
you cannot have information without data.
—Daniel Keys Moran

The most basic of all human needs is the need
to understand and be understood. The best way
to understand people is to listen to them.
—Dr. Ralph Nichols

To answer before listening—that is folly and shame.
—Proverb

The problem is not the problem. The problem is your
attitude about the problem. Do you understand?
—Captain Jack Sparrow

If you want to harness the power of putting
your customers at the center of your business,
you have to start with a complete picture of
who they are and what they want from you.
—Harley Manning and Kerry Bodine

Introduction

F ailure.

Patrick was over three years into his career, and failure was the only word he could use to describe how his efforts at scaling LUCK had gone so far.

He had experienced success applying LUCK in building individual relationships with his colleagues and with the few customers with which he worked. Teammates regularly reported that Patrick understood them far better than others in the organization. As a result, he frequently found himself tasked to work on projects that brought different teams together, which raised his profile to the management team. Within a short time, he had seen enough success with the principles that he had been asked to deliver LUCK training, and some managers had approached him requesting that he mentor employees on their teams. But up to that point, success was limited to working on one-on-one relationships or with small teams; he had not been able to scale it to the thousands of employees in the company and the many more times that number of customers. In fact, in some cases, trying to scale LUCK may have been detrimental.

Patrick had gotten involved in every initiative associated with listening that he could find. He had been a part of focus groups and survey research projects, worked with customers to understand their experiences with the company's products, participated in selecting new software tools, worked with the company's financial analysts, and had even talked the management team into investing in some projects on his own initiative.

But after all of the time he had invested, Patrick knew his approach was not working. It had become more time-consuming to manage customers now than it had been before. Even worse, many employees professed it was faster and easier to find the information they needed to get their jobs done by using the old paper-based filing system than it was by using the new software Patrick had helped to select.

So after three years of trying just the first step of LUCK, Patrick began to question whether any of it could be scaled. Did it really only apply to interpersonal and very small business relationships? Would attempting to scale this small-town principle to a large corporation always ultimately meet with failure? Should he drop his vision for scaling LUCK so he could focus on building a safer and more secure career path?

He stopped by a nearby coffee shop on his way into work that morning. As he opened the door and walked in, the aroma of the freshly brewed coffee instantly transported him over the miles and years back to The Lion's Den during his first year of college and to one of his first lessons on listening.

Infographic

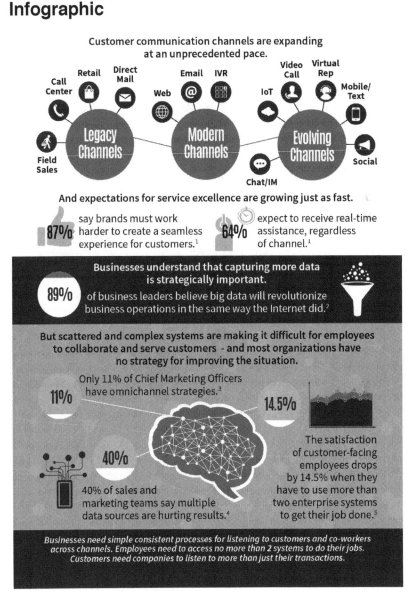

Customer communication channels are expanding at an unprecedented pace.

And expectations for service excellence are growing just as fast.

87% say brands must work harder to create a seamless experience for customers.[1]

64% expect to receive real-time assistance, regardless of channel.[1]

Businesses understand that capturing more data is strategically important.

89% of business leaders believe big data will revolutionize business operations in the same way the Internet did.[2]

But scattered and complex systems are making it difficult for employees to collaborate and serve customers - and most organizations have no strategy for improving the situation.

11% Only 11% of Chief Marketing Officers have omnichannel strategies.[3]

40% 40% of sales and marketing teams say multiple data sources are hurting results.[4]

14.5% The satisfaction of customer-facing employees drops by 14.5% when they have to use more than two enterprise systems to get their job done.[5]

Businesses need simple consistent processes for listening to customers and co-workers across channels. Employees need to access no more than 2 systems to do their jobs. Customers need companies to listen to more than just their transactions.

Download the full Infographic at: www.theLUCKprinciple.com/gotBook

In The Lion's Den

"Good morning, Stranger." Aunt Mal refilled one of her handmade pottery mugs sitting in front of the customer.

Bert Patterson was anything but a stranger, and the mug in front of him was a gift from Aunt Mal. He had first appeared in January, and he had been a fixture in The Lion's Den just about every morning for the past few months. Aunt Mal had nicknamed him "Stranger" just a few days after he had appeared, and it had stuck. It was late in the morning; Bert's second cup of coffee was steaming in the cool air near the front window as he busily typed away on his computer.

"Thanks, Auntie M." Bert had given Aunt Mal her own nickname in return, and he smiled up at her from his work as she filled the cup. In those few months since he first appeared, Bert had changed from a tense and sometimes intimidating figure into someone they all looked forward to seeing each morning.

It was the pre-lunch lull in the shop, and Patrick and Lauren were on the opposite end of the bar talking about his classes. Although he had chosen to focus on engineering, Patrick told his mother that he enjoyed his public speaking and business writing classes more than he had expected.

"That's terrific, sweetie," Lauren responded. "Schools are so good about teaching people to talk. It's too bad they don't have any courses on listening."

"Well, I think that everyone is born knowing how to listen, Mom," Patrick scoffed.

"Is that a fact?" Aunt Mal's voice startled Patrick. She had walked up behind him and overheard the conversation, which was one of her uncanny abilities. "We spend a lot more time listening than we do talking, and the good Lord saw fit to give us two ears and only one mouth. The fact is, most people stink at listening!"

"Look at this, Patrick," Lauren said as she pulled her LUCK journal from behind the counter and flipped it open to a ragged-edged page full of tiny words. "Many years ago, I started writing down all the different ways that people communicate. There are hundreds of ways people communicate without using words. You may think that listening is simply hearing what people say, but it is so much more. Some of the most important things to listen for are the things that are never put into words."

"Take Bert over there for example," Aunt Mal broke back in. "We didn't know a thing about him when he first showed up here a few months ago. He didn't say much, so I really had to listen closely to hear his story.

"When he walked in the first day, he ordered a cup of coffee and sat down, his luggage sitting beside him. I asked him a few questions and found out he needed a place to stay. After a few more questions, I found out that he had taken the bus to town and didn't have a car, so he would need a place nearby. Because he took the bus, it was pretty safe to assume that he didn't want to spend a lot of money. I helped him find an inexpensive apartment just a short way away that was usually vacant at that time of year. He's been coming in here for the first half of his day to work on his book ever since.

"One thing quickly became clear—he was troubled by something. I tried to ask a few questions to start a conversation about whatever was on his mind, but he never engaged. Although he spent about his first hour here every morning talking to different people, he mostly asked questions and offered very little information about himself. But I was able to learn that he was writing a book, a story that takes place in a beach town. He had come here for inspiration but also to gather information to make the story as real as possible.

"So I decided to spend a few minutes with him each day, answering his questions and educating him about the history and landmarks of the area. He was grateful. Yet something was clearly still troubling him.

"Then his wife, Judy, came to visit. I learned from her that they owned a business together. They love it, but they don't make a lot of money. They only have one car, and there was no way that both of them could take much time off. She knew Bert's dream was to write books, so she made him go away to work on it while she held down the business. Bert would have never even suggested something like this, but Judy had insisted."

Patrick recalled how Aunt Mal and Judy had really hit it off. They seemed to be cast from a unique mold of not caring what anyone thought of them while still caring deeply *for* people. It took a while for people to get to know them, and it took them a while to let people in, but once they became your friends, they would do anything for you.

"I also learned from Judy," Aunt Mal continued, "that this was Bert's first book. That's when I connected the dots. Bert wanted this book to be a success. Not just because he wanted to write a good book, but also because he wanted to make Judy's sacrifice worth it.

"So I connected him one of my friends at the university who is an English professor and a published author. He agreed to provide Bert with some feedback and even to have a few of his graduate students do some free editing. Bert changed almost overnight. A few weeks later he thanked me and opened up enough to tell me he was making much better progress because he wasn't as worried as he had been.

"Listening to Bert meant taking in a lot more than what he said aloud. Noticing the luggage he brought was a start. I also tried different approaches to see what he would respond to. I had to listen to those who knew him better than me. I had to remember all of those things, so I could do more with them than just listen; each thing I heard and remembered became a piece of the puzzle.

"Even the way you talk can change how you listen. You and your mother have the same cadence in your speech. But did you know that your mother didn't always talk that way?"

Lauren pressed her lips together and looked away a bit shyly—she was never comfortable with other people praising her.

"Your mother was very intentional about developing her patient way of speaking because she knew it would draw others out and give her the ability to listen to them better. The habit was passed down to you. You'll be a good listener for the rest of your life because of what your mother built into herself," Aunt Mal concluded.

"And you can't keep everything you hear in your head," Lauren added. "I used to have a lot of places where I would write things I learned about LUCK—notebooks, the back of envelopes, and scraps of paper from around the coffee shop. But that didn't work well. It was like I had five different brains for remembering things. Then I couldn't remember which brain I had put something in! It was frustrating and wasted a lot of time. So I eventually created my LUCK journal," she said with a smile. "And the same is true of other things, like a single place to track tasks and appointments. You've got to make it simple to find what you're looking for."

Judy came to pick Bert up just before the tourism season started that summer. A few months later, a box arrived from Bert. It was filled with copies of his first book, titled *In The Lion's Den*. They were thrilled to find that it was filled with fictionalized stories about them. Although the book wasn't a bestseller, Lauren made a point of always keeping some available for sale in the shop and giving free copies away to regular customers. It added something unique to the little shop, and it brought tourists, students, and others back year after year. Every year after that, Bert and Judy returned for at least a week and spent most mornings at the coffee shop.

Many years later, Bert would do something that would forever change the coffee shop.

Field Trip

Patrick wasn't ready to give up trying to scale The LUCK Principle, but he also realized that he was in over his head. If he was going to be successful, he would need help. With this in mind, he resolved to build a new way of listening into his career. At least once each year, he decided, he would take a field trip with the purpose of learning the secrets of successful businesses and what role—if any—LUCK played in success.

Patrick learned that a company in his city had been voted by its employees as one of the best places to work in the country. Upon further investigation, he also found they had an outstanding reputation for customer service. Patrick placed a call to the head of human resources, who directed him to a person with a title he had never heard before: chief people officer. The CPO enthusiastically spent a few hours with Patrick.

"From very early on, we knew our business was about one thing: people," The CPO launched into the discussion before Patrick could ask the first question. "First, about customers—the people outside of our company. Second, about employees—the people inside of our company. With that simple philosophy, we experienced years of success. Our people naturally collaborated to serve our customers. But ten years ago it stopped working. People working together was actually working against our business." This comment threw a wrench in Patrick's expectations of how the story would unfold.

"How," he asked, "could working together well hurt your people and your business?"

"Let me explain it this way," the CPO began. "About two years ago, I witnessed a horrible car accident. I was turning out of a parking area that was being repaved. Some of the workers were wearing green safety vests and were trying to direct traffic at a busy four-way intersection, which had two lanes of traffic each way. They tried to work together with one another and with the traffic, but one of them ended up signaling a car to turn while the other was signaling traffic to continue through the intersection. The result was horrifying. They were well intentioned, but just because they had a bright green safety vest on didn't mean they knew what they were doing. Everyone would have been better off if no one had been directing traffic at all.

"And we were seeing that kind of story play out in our business time and time again. The way you work together as a small company becomes horribly inefficient or even counterproductive when you grow," he continued. "What worked well for us as a smaller company didn't scale. When we first tried the latest tools for collaboration and relationship management, we found they made the problems worse. Those tools were our green vests—it made us feel like we knew what we were doing, but we didn't."

Now he had Patrick's full attention. This sounded exactly like what Patrick was experiencing.

"Let me back up and start from the beginning. We were a successful small business with about seventy-five employees in a single location. However, when we expanded to seven global production plants, numerous smaller locations, and over a thousand employees and were working across channels for distribution, retail, and web purchasing, things changed. Our people spent an extraordinary amount of time trying to track or find the information they needed just to do their jobs. We frequently found ourselves asking customers to repeat themselves or made redundant internal decisions and rediscovered old information because we had no way of documenting it or making it easy to find. Although we paid competitive salaries and provided solid benefits, we had a lot of unhappy people who could not work efficiently, so they had to work extra hours or do a poor job. We became trapped in a vicious cycle, and we couldn't scale our business—the only way to solve these problems was to add people, which added more complexity and made the problems worse. The vital signs of our organization—profit, revenue, new client growth, and customer and employee satisfaction—had been rising rapidly but were now plateauing."

Patrick briefly described The LUCK Principle. He initially described how LUCK applies to individual relationships, as he had learned in the coffee shop. Then he explained how LUCK could be scaled to work in a larger business setting.

"*Listening* is about hearing what customers and employees are saying, and capturing that in a corporate memory—one place where everyone can go to find information, data, and content. *Understanding* is about giving the team the tools they need to analyze what is in the corporate memory to motivate insights and inspire better decisions. Some may need information on a single customer or a single document at a time, and others may need to analyze information in aggregate. *Connecting* is about the processes for transforming those insights into actions—into a better customer experience. *Knowing* is about collaborating as a team to constantly track the results, make improvements, and discover innovations. If I were to boil it down to one sentence, I would say LUCK is about using data, analysis, process, and lessons learned to create better relationships."

The CPO looked at Patrick for a long moment, and then asked, "What's your plan?" The blank look Patrick gave him was all the answer he needed.

"I like your idea of LUCK, Patrick, and I think it has always been in our DNA. We hired and mentored people to be good at listening to one another, and to customers, and to work together well. So LUCK is in the head of most of the people who work here. But you need more than an idea, you need a clear vision and a plan. I think you're in a similar place to where we were about six months after we got started down this road, so I think you can learn a lot from our experience." Patrick winced, thinking over the past three years that his company had been struggling with this.

"It comes down to two things," the CPO continued. "First, you're smart to be talking to others. We took too many years to get this right. I wish we had researched this and built a better roadmap before we started—maybe looking five years out. We could have reduced costs, decreased frustration, and gotten to where we are now many years ahead of what it ultimately took. Instead, we spent years feeling like we were wandering without direction until all the pieces came together. With a better vision of the destination, the journey would have certainly been faster and smoother. Another thing we learned on the journey was to spend more time 'riding along'—actually experiencing a day in the lives of our customers and our employees in their journeys. We developed a lot of innovations by listening to them this way. You need a plan—the clearer, the better—and your customers and coworkers better be involved in developing such a plan.

"The second part involves thinking a little more deeply about how you build what you call the 'corporate memory.' It's a process that I call 'elimination, integration, and migration,' or 'less is more,'" he went on. "Technology is wonderful, but too much technology can prove a burden. We found that if we asked any of our people to use more than a couple of systems to get their jobs done, it actually slowed them down. After we rolled out a new system that showed a lot of promise, one of our people commented, 'I feel like I'm trying to climb a mountain with a heavy pack, and you just threw in another rock and said it should be easier now!' That statement was the slap in the face that our leadership team needed.

"We did a bit of research and found that our employees sometimes used more than twenty software packages to get their jobs done. Every time we had another problem, we ran out and bought another piece of technology to solve it. Learning and navigating all those systems to enter information and find the information became incredibly time consuming. Technology should be made to work for employees, not the other way around. Employees spend too much time working for technology when employers invest too little in setting the technology up. This sends a message to employees that technology is more valuable than they are. We were not only destroying productivity but also decimating employee morale!

"The complexity of data and the number of places to capture it will always increase. But the simplicity of capturing and accessing data can be improved for employees. We achieved this through elimination, integration, and migration. Elimination means completely dropping some systems and migrating the functionality to another system. Integration means sharing data between systems. Migration means migrating some functionality from one system to another system. Together, these steps help create fewer systems that our teams have to use to get their jobs done. After we did this, we saw improvements in productivity and scalability—and job satisfaction began to rise again."

"Why," asked Patrick, "did you wait so long before elimination, integration, and migration?"

"Well, again," responded the CPO, "we shouldn't have waited so long. One big problem was that we kept getting talked into believing new software would get us where we wanted to go. That's about the same as putting a race car onto a path made for a mule and expecting a better result. It was worse than getting us nowhere—it created more systems that added complexity and problems that had to be fixed later. The second problem was what I mentioned earlier—the lack of a roadmap—so we didn't know if or when we would need additional systems and how they should fit with existing systems. The third issue arose from our own thinking—we were so far in the box of doing things the way we always had, with systems that had worked for us in the past, that it took a lot of pain to convince us to try something new.

"But all of these issues were really just symptoms of a larger underlying problem." The CPO began to wrap up. "The real problem was in our approach. You can't solve a problem using the same approach that created the problem. We had to transform from a company that focused on scaling how we *transact* into a company that scales how we *interact* and discover insights. We needed a new perspective, and this is one of the reasons why my position was created and why we invested in fresh perspectives from outside of the company".

Journal Entry

LISTEN

ALL RELATIONSHIPS ARE BUILT ON THE FOUNDATION OF LISTENING AND
ACCESSING THE MEMORY OF WHAT IS LEARNED.

IN BUSINESS, MEMORY IS ABOUT DATA. BUT THERE IS SO MUCH DATA, COMING
FROM AND BEING STORED IN SO MANY DIFFERENT PLACES, ACCESSING
MEMORY IS INCREASINGLY COMPLEX.

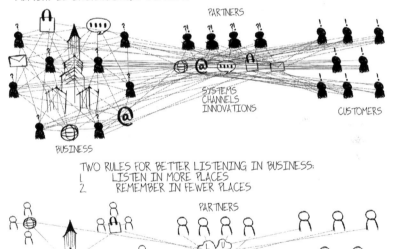

What's the Application?

"That's nice, but what's the application?" The challenging words Aunt Mal had said again and again stuck in his mind for the rest of his life. She meant that acquiring new knowledge is meaningless unless you let it challenge you and unless you take the time to pause and plan out how it will change you. "If you don't apply it, then it's just nice, and nice is just a waste of time." Every time Patrick learned something new, he would be haunted by that voice until he found a way to apply the knowledge.

His company didn't have the roadmap that the CPO had mentioned, so this is where Patrick started. As Patrick did more research on how to plan for this kind of initiative, his team discovered an idea called the 40/20/40 principle. The team found that organizations often make the mistake of investing most of their time and budget on buying and setting up technology—maybe 80 percent of their resources are invested there and only 20 percent on planning and change management. The approach Patrick's company applied put the emphasis on planning (perhaps 40 percent) and on project controls and change management (perhaps another 40 percent). Using this approach, they more frequently reached their goals and sustained change over the long-term, and the 20 percent invested in technology was much more effective. Patrick applied 40/20/40 thinking to a master roadmap that he continuously refined for many years, and to each subsequent phase of the project.

As the company began the planning process, Patrick realized that it was making the same mistake Lauren had made—it had too many brains. Every year the organization came up with a new way to listen to customers and coworkers, and to address this it seemed like every year, it added another system for capturing new data. Just like Lauren had consolidated her note taking into the LUCK journal, Patrick's company needed to migrate, integrate, and eliminate to create a smaller number of places the teams had to go to find what they were looking for. They could always add new ears—new ways to listen—but the information needed to find its way into fewer brains so there were fewer places people needed to go to find information.

Patrick focused much of his time on an internal campaign that he dubbed "Single-Minded" in an effort to simplify the lives of his colleagues. His goal was to craft a system in which teams would have to go to fewer places to track and find the information they needed to get their jobs done and to serve customers, while at the same time retaining an ability to listen across an ever larger number of channels and systems.

What Patrick did not yet know was that having a good memory did not mean the team would use it. He and his company would have to learn that lesson soon enough.

CHAPTER 2
UNDERSTAND

Most people listen with the intent
to reply, not to understand.
—Stephen R. Covey

Be nice to geeks, you'll probably end up working for one.
—Bill Gates

Data are just summaries of thousands of stories.
—Chip and Dan Heath

Listening to the data is important…but so is experience
and intuition. After all, what is intuition at its
best but large amounts of data of all kinds filtered
through a human brain rather than a math model?
—Steve Lohr

In the business world, the rearview mirror
is always clearer than the windshield.
—Warren Buffett

Introduction

B ig data.

Patrick had done such a good job getting his organization to rally around listening to customers that now, almost seven years into his career, he had created a new problem. Three things had become clear to him: (1) the organization had access to a tremendous amount of data, (2) this data had not led to significant new insights, understanding, actions, or results, and (3) no one else seemed to appreciate the opportunities missed.

The bottom line was that the organization had slowly bought into Patrick's idea of listening, but teams were showing little in the way of results. So far, Patrick had mostly stayed below the radar. He remained fairly junior in the organization, and most of the pressure he felt was pressure he put on himself. But that changed in a one-on-one meeting with his manager.

"Patrick, the CEO has asked us to present a plan for working with big data to her senior leadership team at the next quarterly meeting. You've been one of the big advocates for creating all of this data, so I want you to prepare and present the recommendations."

This created a great opportunity for Patrick, but he was anxious. He had some ideas of how big data fit into The LUCK Principle, but none of them seemed quite right. He had worked with the IT department to set up some reporting and dashboard systems. They were pretty slick, but usage and impact had been limited because there always seemed to be underlying problems with the data. Patrick knew their untapped data was like a goldmine if they could only learn how to use it more effectively to innovate and serve customers better.

He began to twirl his pen in his hand—a habit he had developed whenever deep in thought. His mind turned back to The Lion's Den all those years ago. How could the way his mother understood people parallel what Patrick was experiencing now?

Infographic

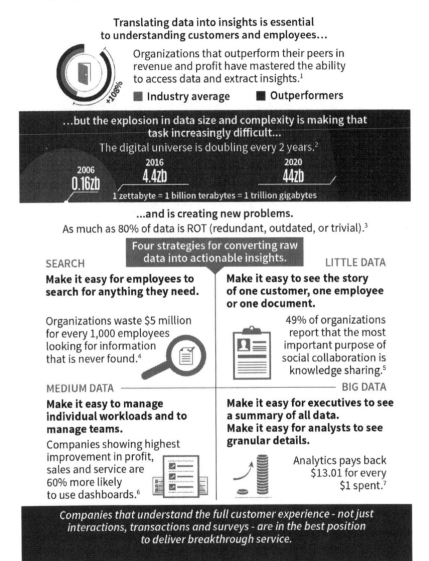

Translating data into insights is essential to understanding customers and employees...

Organizations that outperform their peers in revenue and profit have mastered the ability to access data and extract insights.[1]

■ Industry average   ■ Outperformers

...but the explosion in data size and complexity is making that task increasingly difficult...

The digital universe is doubling every 2 years.[2]

2006	2016	2020
0.16zb	4.4zb	44zb

1 zettabyte = 1 billion terabytes = 1 trillion gigabytes

...and is creating new problems.

As much as 80% of data is ROT (redundant, outdated, or trivial).[3]

Four strategies for converting raw data into actionable insights.

SEARCH

Make it easy for employees to search for anything they need.

Organizations waste $5 million for every 1,000 employees looking for information that is never found.[4]

LITTLE DATA

Make it easy to see the story of one customer, one employee or one document.

49% of organizations report that the most important purpose of social collaboration is knowledge sharing.[5]

MEDIUM DATA

Make it easy to manage individual workloads and to manage teams.

Companies showing highest improvement in profit, sales and service are 60% more likely to use dashboards.[6]

BIG DATA

Make it easy for executives to see a summary of all data.
Make it easy for analysts to see granular details.

Analytics pays back $13.01 for every $1 spent.[7]

Companies that understand the full customer experience - not just interactions, transactions and surveys - are in the best position to deliver breakthrough service.

Download the full Infographic at: www.theLUCKprinciple.com/gotBook

In The Lion's Den

"There is a dangerous gap that exists between oneself and others," Patrick's mother Lauren said. "We can't really cross the gap until we understand the other person. Some people go charging right into the gap and often make a wreck of themselves and others, even if they have good intentions. Others build bridges but never have the courage to cross them. Understanding is all about building the bridge; connecting is about crossing it.

"Look at Ann, for example."

Ann had worked at the shop for two years and was in her last year of college. Patrick knew Ann was a great part of the team. She seemed to be a natural with practicing LUCK—she engaged well with customers and coworkers, taking a genuine interest in them. A fantastic barista, she made great coffee and even developed new processes that helped everyone work together better. In fact, she had already grown to be better at this than Patrick, and he had been helping in the shop since he was eleven years old. Ann was behind the counter and had just finished taking an order from a customer.

"Ann will leave when she graduates in about five months. Not only will we lose a great part of our team, but also I don't think that Ann will be as happy working in a cube at a big company in a city as she is right here. It's time for me to help her see that."

Patrick could not pretend that he was not more than a little surprised at his mother's words. How could she know what was best for Ann? They went back to work helping to deal with the morning crowd. Later that morning, when things slowed down, Lauren invited Patrick and Ann to sit down with her in front of the fireplace on the second floor of the shop.

"Ann, I want to thank you," started Lauren. "You always do a great job. But I was really impressed with your knowledge and excitement about wine last night. Everything from your tasting notes, to the regional maps, to the way you helped us to appreciate the subtle flavors in each wine—you really educated me and your classmates quite a bit."

"Thank you." Ann blushed at the compliment.

Ann took a class called Wines and Vines at the university, and she had invited a few classmates and Lauren to do a tasting at the coffee shop the previous evening.

"This is clearly more than just a class for you. I've been thinking that we should include a small wine bar as part of our pub. Could I ask you to head that effort up? You'll need to decide what equipment to purchase, work with the distributors to determine what wines to carry, and develop a marketing plan. Would you be willing to do that?"

Ann's face lit up in a way Patrick had never seen it. Ann always maintained a lot of energy and a positive attitude about the sometimes mundane work at the coffee shop. This was different. Her expression made it seem as if she had just unwrapped the Christmas present she had always quietly wanted.

"Of course…I'd love to…thank you Miss Lauren!" she exclaimed, and she threw her arms around Patrick's mother.

Ann came from a small town in Georgia and had been raised to call adults by their first name, preceded by "Miss" or "Mister." Patrick liked the mixture of respect and familiarity that addressing people this way communicated, and Ann's Southern accent added the perfect measure of warmth to it. This was part of Ann's magic with customers—particularly the tourists who came primarily from the Northeast and were fascinated by Ann's near perfect Southern charm. Patrick wondered if part of his mother's care for Ann originated from how much the two of them were alike.

Over the next few months, the wine bar became as much a part of The Lion's Den as the pub section, and Ann tirelessly worked to make it an even bigger part. She held educational seminars and wine tastings weekly. She patiently worked with customers to help them develop an appreciation for the subtle nuances among the different wines. She collaborated with the other employees to train them on the basics of wine. Some of The Lion's Den customers became wine enthusiasts. Additionally, a number of new customers began to become regulars.

It was late one evening, just a month before graduation. Ann, Patrick, and Lauren had been working together to close the shop down.

"Patrick, can you finish up? Ann, can I speak to you for a few minutes before you head home?" asked Lauren.

They sat down at a table opposite the coffee bar. Patrick listened to their discussion as he finished cleaning up and cashing out the register. Aunt Mal had brought in some new photos and paintings to replace the ones that had been sold in the last few months. She buzzed around the shop, hanging and adjusting the new artwork.

"Ann, I couldn't be any happier with the job you've done with the wine bar here. It has transformed our little business, there's no other word for it. When you graduate, I'd like you to consider staying here to take the wine bar to the next level." Her words, clear and intentional—much more so than usual—made it seem as if she were unaware of how ridiculous the idea was. Patrick knew immediately that this was uncomfortable for his mother, and she must have been preparing for this moment for a long time.

"Miss Lauren…I couldn't possibly," caught off guard, Ann stammered out her reply. "You've been so good to me, but…I've spent the last four years getting ready for a technology job. It's what I'm supposed to do next. I'm so sorry, but I couldn't possibly."

"Ann, you did an internship for a technology company, didn't you? What did you think about that?" prompted Lauren.

"It was a management-consulting and technology-implementation company. Not so bad. They told me I was one of the best interns they'd ever had. They even offered me a job, so I guess it was a pretty good experience. But I've decided to go work for a larger company. More room to grow, you know."

"Ann, Ann…listen to yourself," started Lauren. "Are you going to settle for 'it wasn't bad' and 'I guess it was pretty good'? You think you need to settle for a job because it's where you've told yourself the future is. What will you think when you wake up ten years from now and find yourself sitting in front a computer and going to meetings all day long?"

Ann felt cornered by the diminutive yet determined Lauren. At the same time, her deep respect for Lauren kept her open to listening, and the words stirred hopes and fears that Ann hadn't realized were there. She fought to control her emotions, but her jaw clenched and she shifted in her seat—Ann felt vulnerable and exposed and she wanted to protect herself.

"People like Patrick find that kind of work engaging, but it's not for you," Lauren continued. "I've seen you working with wine, customers, and coworkers in this small town business. It engages your entire mind and soul. You have such a joy for it that you can work tirelessly on top of your studies and still do it well. Ann, I can tell you that you are not going to be happy if you're stuck at a desk job, rarely working with customers and never working with wine. You may not know it about yourself yet, but I know it. I'm offering you something that may be frightening. You can take the other path, but by the time you realize you're unhappy, it may be almost impossible to turn back.

"Sweetie." Lauren reached across the table, her voice softening but still confident, and took both of Ann's hands in her own. "You know I don't believe in all of that 'follow your passion' stuff—everyone in the world would be a surfer or an artist if that were true." Patrick saw Aunt Mal grimace as she was adjusting a new painting next to their table. "But you have two great alternatives. Maybe you're just not giving yourself permission to think big enough about what else you can do. The bookstore next door is closing down at the end of this summer. The building will be put up for sale. We can set up an amazing wine shop in there, and you can manage it. If you do well with it, then we can talk about a partnership. It won't be easy. You'll have to earn every bit of it and work harder than you would ever have to work in any computer job, but you could be majority owner of the shop in time."

Helping someone else to start in business wasn't unprecedented for Patrick's mother. Lauren was part owner of another business with Aunt Mal, and Patrick knew she had at least discussed various options with others.

Ann sat and looked from Lauren, to the table, to Lauren again. Bewildered.

"It's a lot to take in, I know. Think on it for a while. No matter what you do, I'll be your biggest cheerleader."

That evening, Lauren and Patrick discussed Ann, wine, and how to understand people.

"If you can understand the things about people that they don't say," started Lauren, "then you're in a great position to serve them." Lauren talked about how Ann didn't really know some things about herself that Lauren intuited, and Lauren wanted to help Ann in those areas.

"The best way to tell what someone is going to do in the future is to see what they've done in the past. What they have done and how they have done it tells you more about what they will do than what they tell you or what some test says they should do. Past behavior reveals more about someone's future than anything else. I know a lot of things about Ann. I know what gets her excited. I know what she is good at. I know what she will work hard for. I know what bores her. And I know things about this town, the people in it, and how those things might connect to Ann. Taking the time to not just listen to Ann, but to really understand her, built a bridge between us. So I took a risk and crossed the bridge—I think it will work out pretty well for her.

"Just like our car," Lauren continued, "we all have a God-given dashboard. Emotions, feelings and feedback that tell us how we're doing with our inner world and our outer world. Exhaustion tells us we need a rest, anxiety may be telling us we're on the wrong road, and social intelligence helps us to understand and connect with others. Sometimes we ignore our own gauges, and in the worst case, sometimes we've ripped out the wiring to try to protect ourselves. Feedback from people around us is a part of our dashboard to help us read the gauges that we may be ignoring."

Ann decided to stay on and work for Lauren, but she was careful to say it would be a one-year experiment. During that year, Patrick saw Ann's store, From Vine to Wine, flourish. It shared a back deck with The Lion's Den where live music played in the evenings from spring through fall. Ann's skills with computers and marketing proved a big boost to both of the shops.

Field Trip

All these years after the coffee shop, the parallels for scaling understanding from the individual level to the business level remained unclear to Patrick. Big data, which Patrick thought was key to understanding customers, was more corporate and cold; it just couldn't parallel the depth of individual relationships.

Ding…ding…ding!

The sound of someone trying to reach him through his company's instant messaging application snapped Patrick out of his reflections on lessons learned in the coffee shop.

"Patrick, this is Tom, over in marketing." Patrick had not yet met Tom Kelly, the new executive vice president of marketing, but he could see his information on his screen.

"I heard you're spearheading the big data recommendations to the senior leadership team, and I was hoping I could partner with you. The internal articles you've published on LUCK are great—an interesting convergence of ideas that are both obvious but revolutionary in business. It seems like you've not only put a lot of effort into learning about data, but you're also well connected to the others working on this inside and outside of the company. And I love your idea of field trips and what you've already been learning from those." Patrick was impressed—Tom had done his homework. In his first few weeks, he had already done his research on Patrick through his internal online profile and had learned a lot about the contributions he had been making.

"Inspired by your field trips, I've arranged one myself. I'd like you to come with me to meet the head of global marketing at one of our most important suppliers."

Two weeks later he and Tom sat in the office of Kutloisiso Naidoo in Bonn, Germany.

"Thank you, Ms. Naidoo, for agreeing to meet with us to share some of your experiences with how you have used big data to forge such strong relationships with your customers," started Tom. "Your organization has been lauded as one of the most customer-centric in the world, which is consistent with our own experience. Our operations people report that no one even comes close to understanding our needs the way you understand them, nor is any other company as easy and efficient to work with. Our sales team tells us that you're so intrinsic to the growth our company has experienced that your organization is an inseparable part of the team. Even if it means collaborating with other suppliers, your team does what they need to do to make us successful."

"*Bitte*, and please call me Lori," she responded. Although she used some German words, she spoke in a melodious and engaging South African accent and occasionally used colloquialisms from her home country as well. When she made introductions and shook hands, she smiled in a casual way that immediately dispelled any formality and put Tom and Patrick at ease. "But I must start by pointing out you may be asking the wrong question. Big data is not of much help until you have mastered little data and medium data." Lori paused, and from the expression on both Patrick's and Tom's faces, she could see more explanation was needed.

"The big problem is not big data. The big problem is little data. Little data is the foundation for big data. And little data should be enriched with big data," Lori began. "Like you, I was drawn to big data as a way to understand customers. As a marketer, I want to find new insights that I can apply to large groups of customers at once. But you cannot have big data without having little data first.

And they exist in a circular relationship. Little data feeds big data; what you learn when you bring data together as big data then feeds back into little data so everyone collaborates in creating and using knowledge. You cannot have a herd without first having a single gazelle. But once a gazelle is in a herd, it is changed and improved by being a part of the herd, and the herd itself is changed and improved because the gazelle is a part of it. It is the same with little data and big data. Let me help you understand how we view this."

Patrick was scribbling notes at a furious pace, but was still struggling to keep up. The vision of little data not just contributing to big data, but being itself enhanced by big data about a customer from other sources around the company, brought to mind how his mother had been able to form a complete picture of Ann.

"Little data is the story of a single person—a single customer, employee, or even a single idea, transaction, or document. Every time we interact with someone, we need the right information about their story at our fingertips. So, therefore, little data is for people on the front lines who are interacting directly with other people and need to quickly see insights and make decisions. Some call this the 360-degree view."

As Lori spoke, Patrick recalled how Tom was able to access his story to better partner with him as an employee, but he also recalled how time-consuming it was for their frontline employees to get full information on an individual customer.

"Oftentimes," Lori continued, "our people only need a small part of that view to make a specific decision—such as a specific transaction that may predict something else a customer is likely to need or knowledge about the support record of a product with which they are experiencing issues.

"Big data is the story of all customers or employees. We build it by bringing together little data from many different places. Some of this is from accounting, some from marketing and sales, some even from Internet-connected equipment we have installed at customer locations like yours. With it, we find insights and develop new innovations based on what we know about large groups of people. But we also use it to enrich little data. For example, in my marketing department, we often find new insights that we then send back to our little-data systems to help customer-facing employees make better decisions; as another example, our accounting department collects information about orders and payments that sales can see in their little-data system. Analysts in our organization have access to the deepest, richest, and most complex pool of big data. Executives also access big data, but this is in the form of high-level summaries they can use to quickly spot trends and to run the business."

Tom spent some time asking Lori questions and digging more deeply into the role that marketing played. During their dialog it became clear to Patrick that, because of the central role marketing played with both employee and customer communications, Tom's marketing department was going to have to become much more tech-savvy and analytical than had been necessary in the past.

"Medium data," Lori continued after concluding the discussion with Tom, "is what is used to help manage workloads at the individual and team level. Most of the time it comes from the same systems that have little data, but it is in the form of summaries that managers and teams can use to monitor their progress and find ways to make improvements. So medium data is mostly used by managers and the individuals they manage." An image of the personal dashboards that Patrick's mother described flashed through his head, the parallel concept of individuals and teams needing dashboards in the workplace made perfect sense. It wasn't lost on Patrick that the situation in his company was more like driving a car with an out-of-date paper roadmap rather than with a GPS device.

"We spent a lot of time gathering all of this data, and one thing we found is the most critical data is always past history. What individuals have done in the past remains the best way to predict what they will do in the future, a better predictor than what they tell us on a survey, what data can be purchased about them, or what a rep thinks they will do. So we work very hard to make past history, and predictive analytics based on this history, available in little-data and big-data systems. In this way, we adjust to serve the customer in the best possible manner." Now Patrick remembered his coffee shop lesson about a person's past being the best way to predict their future.

"Ultimately, we want to connect with customers and with one another in the best possible manner," Lori moved to conclude, "which is the 'C' in your LUCK Principle. You see, we have discovered that we should strive to do the right thing for the long-term needs of the customer—which isn't always the best thing for our short-term revenue. But we cannot do that in a meaningful way unless we first store everything we can in little-data systems and then distribute that knowledge to everyone who works with people and makes decisions about people across the organization. Without that, we are making decisions based on guesswork and hunches."

"I think I'm following you," Tom said after a moment. "It sounds as if you're saying the data you have about your customers is like a building. The executives need to know a little bit about everything going on throughout the building—a summary of production on each floor. Analysts need to know a lot about everything going on in the building—they need to analyze the activities of every individual in the building. Those are two different types of big data. Employees on the front lines need to know a great deal about specific individuals within the building—that's little data. And managers need to view a summary of what their teams see and do—perhaps a detailed summary of what is going on within one or two floors of the building. That's medium data."

"Excellent!" said Lori. "I couldn't have phrased it better myself. But also remember that all of those people need to be able to search all the data and find what they need quickly. We found that the more data we created, the longer it took our people to sift through it. We consumed a tremendous amount of time just searching for the information needed to make a decision or to get a job done. Just because you have data doesn't mean you can find the specific items you need quickly."

"Of course!" Patrick was so excited, he hadn't realized that he had said this aloud until he noticed Lori and Tom staring at him. He explained that this had been one of the missing ingredients. For his mother, searching for information was seamless because it happened inside her head—but with a large group of employees, a company needed better tools for searching the corporate memory.

"That 'corporate memory' as you call it," Lori commented, "became the source of an important innovation for us. As we went deeper with learning how to connect with our customers and one another, we came to realize that most of our technology projects were geared toward the finance, accounting, and manufacturing teams. That approach suited us well for the first part of our history. But we increasingly found ourselves forcing employees to use accounting systems to do tasks that were more aligned to customer and employee relationships. Eventually we came to realize that the most important asset in the twenty-first century—the source of competitive advantage and innovation—is people. As a result, teams that contribute to marketing, employee collaboration, and innovation are playing a bigger leadership role in making decisions about our technology."

They closed with a discussion about the organizational changes Lori's company had undergone in the past five years. She indicated that technology, analysis, innovation, and caring for the customer were no longer the jobs of just a select group of people. Everyone on the team had to develop skills in these areas. "The digital and the human worlds are starting to collide. As a result, the language of business is changing, and technology will soon replace those who do not learn to speak it. We are successfully integrating systems with other systems, unglücklicherweise," Lori concluded, with some sadness in her voice as she momentarily slipped into speaking German, "that is, unfortunately, we are finding it much more difficult to integrate systems with people."

That last comment stunned Patrick, and in her eyes he noted genuine concern. He realized that this wasn't only a warning to him but also an area of deep rooted trepidation Lori had for her own coworkers.

Journal Entry

UNDERSTAND

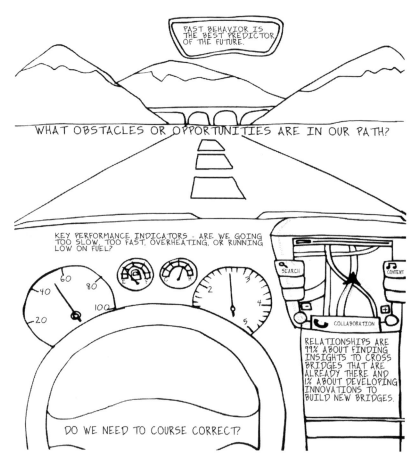

What's the Application?

As Patrick reviewed his notes on the flight home, he could finally envision how the "Understand" principle scaled from individual relationships to work in large organizations. Taking the data gathered in the "Listen" principle and distributing it in the form of little data, medium data, and big data to everyone in the organization so they could search it and identify insights about people proved to be the secret formula for scaling understanding. And as was the case with individual relationships, understanding past actions remained the best predictor of the future.

This process enabled individuals, teams, leadership, and even automated machine-learning systems to develop insights and innovations and to make better decisions. Just as understanding Ann allowed Patrick's mother to make better decisions as she interacted with her, understanding data helps employees better engage with customers and with one another without having to rely on hunches. Armed with a wealth of data about customers, employees could not only engage better with customers, but they could also identify what customers consider valuable—not just for the immediate bottom line of Patrick's company—and thus build longer-lasting relationships based on a level of trust previously unattainable. His mother called this building bridges.

Upon some additional reflection, Patrick grew encouraged because his co-workers had already put many of these pieces in place with how they listened to one another. That's why Tom could search for people such as Patrick who were working on big data projects, learn so much about him, and quickly connect with him to accelerate the mission of the organization. There remained more work to do, but the company already benefitted from the basics of the "Understand" principle.

With this new knowledge, Patrick's presentation on big data was turning into something quite different from what he had anticipated. Their organization acquired a lot of data, but the teams weren't identifying new insights and developing new innovations based on this. Few people on the front lines with customers could see past history, let alone predictions about the future, so they didn't know the best way to help such customers. They had a lot of work to do on little data, training, and even organizational structure if they were ever going to effectively leverage big data.

Getting their company to embrace little data, medium data, and big data would be hard work. Setting up the technology would be difficult, but getting employees to change how they viewed their job would create the biggest challenge. However, there was some good news: The decision they had made as a result of scaling the "Listen" principle, to reduce the number of systems people had to use to listen and get their job done, was going the make the process of understanding much easier than it would have been otherwise. Not only had this decision created a shift in their culture, but also it resulted in a smaller set of systems with which it would be easier to work.

His presentation went well, and a number of new projects were ultimately launched to improve how the organization listened, collaborated on, and developed new insights. Soon after they began this transformation, Tom pulled Patrick aside.

"I think we're working too hard on innovation," he started, excitedly. Then, after seeing Patrick's surprised expression, he quickly continued, "We talk a lot about innovation—about building bridges—and that's good. But one thing we've discovered in the marketing department is that it is expensive and risky to build new bridges—to deliver innovations—so we should be very selective about that. There are hundreds of bridges already built—many ways to connect with people. When we focus too much on new innovation, we often ignore those bridges that already exist. We're starting to view the bigger part of our job working with big data as finding the bridges already there. If we can discover where each person already has bridges, then we can cross them." Tom and Patrick refined this and they began to train their teams on what they called the 99:1 Rule. "In relationships, ninety-nine percent of our time should be spent finding and crossing bridges, one percent of our time should be spent identifying and building new bridges."

It was exciting to be on the executives' radar screens. They were on board with scaling LUCK, and Patrick was enjoying the responsibility that this entailed. However, he knew the team had not yet embraced one of the most fundamental principles that he had learned from his years at the coffee shop—and if he couldn't figure out how to get them there, then all of these efforts would amount to nothing.

CHAPTER 3
CONNECT

We are hard-wired for connections.
—Dr. Brené Brown

*The currency of real networking is
not greed but generosity.*
—Keith Ferrazzi

*[The best salespeople] win by...knowing
their customers' world better than their
customers know it themselves, teaching them
what they don't know, but should.*
—Matthew Dixon

Succeeding in business is all about making connections.
—Richard Branson

*If you can't describe what you are doing as a
process, you don't know what you're doing.*
—W. Edwards Deming

Introduction

I t didn't make Patrick feel any better knowing he had been right about how difficult it would be to get his team to fully embrace the "Understand" principle.

Getting the attention of the executive team had been an important milestone for his LUCK initiatives, and significant progress had been made. Team members listened to customers and one another, and many of them made progress in analyzing the information to develop helpful insights. But they weren't consistently delivering profitable results.

Skilled people had been hired and trained, and were expected to build relationships on top of the foundation of data and analysis that the company had provided. But the two worlds weren't coming together. Instead of adopting new processes that were being introduced, people fell back into old habits. Changes to improve the business were not being sustained.

Now, the executive attention that had been exciting and motivating was starting to cut the other way. The CEO asked tough, probing, questions. Patrick knew it was just a matter of time until she would make his life very uncomfortable if she didn't see more bottom-line returns for the time and money invested.

Patrick had foreseen at least some of the problem coming. But he had no idea of how to get others in the business on board to accomplish what was needed. He also had a nagging sense that he had missed something important. Something that was staring him right in the face.

These things weighed on his mind as he stood in line to order lunch at the sandwich shop across the street from the office. A loud and familiar noise coming from the street outside took him back to another time and place when he had learned one of his earliest lessons about connecting.

Infographic

Person-to-person connections are at the heart of organizational success.

+$83,000 annual revenue — Employees with more connections generated $83,000 more revenue per year.[1]

A small number of positive or negative connectors can make or break a team.

5X — The total lifetime value of a promoter customer is as much as 5x higher than a detractor customer.[2]

54% — Teammates with toxic co-workers are 54% more likely to quit and cost as much as 3x more to replace.[3]

· ·

2 Relationship process misconceptions:

Relationships are not a process.
RESULT: No processes are developed. Relationship practices cannot be repeated, measured, improved or scaled.

Relationships are like other business processes.
RESULT: Relationship processes become restrictive, results are stifled, change is slow.

Profit results are 30% greater for firms using sales process than for those that are not.[4]

average

· ·

If the 5% of the least effective leaders in organizations improve from below - average to average in how they collaborate with others, they will save the other 95% an average of 3.75 hours per week.[5]

Effective customer and employee engagement processes are rigid at the core, flexible at the edges, and have RIMS: repeatable, improvable, measurable, and scalable .

Download the full Infographic at: www.theLUCKprinciple.com/gotBook

In The Lion's Den

It started as a dull rumble, like distant thunder. The noise grew steadily louder until the window panes in the coffee shop rattled. Then they appeared. Dozens of motorcycles poured into the town square and backed into every available parking place. As the bikers dismounted and headed for The Lion's Den, it felt like a high voltage jolt ran through the entire place. The double doors had been left open that day to enjoy the almost perfect weather and fall breeze.

Aunt Mal positioned herself just inside of the door. She stood as straight and tall as Patrick had ever seen, and somehow her diminutive, five-foot frame seemed much larger.

Then the first of the bikers approached. He had pivoted his sunglasses off his eyes as he walked toward the shop, and they now rested on top of his thick red-turning-gray hair. He wore jeans, a faded t-shirt, and a leather vest full of patches. His tattooed arms looked as if they had spent many years doing hard work in the sun. His moustache spread across the top of his expressionless mouth and down to his chin; it faintly resembled the long ape-hanger handlebars on his bike. He towered over Aunt Mal.

The inside of the shop fell completely silent, and the only noise that could be heard outside was the slowly fading sound of motorcycles as the riders swung down their kickstands, switched off their engines, and dismounted.

"Hello, Jimmy," Aunt Mal said in an almost defiant voice.

"Hello, Mal," the biker responded flatly.

And then, in an instant, Aunt Mal wrapped her arms around Jimmy's neck, her feet off the ground. They embraced in a bear hug, both with huge grins on their faces.

Lauren strode past both of them and yelled, "Come on in folks— we've been preparing for you for weeks! The beer is cold, and the band is warming up!"

Just a few minutes later, The Lion's Den teemed with a group of the most rugged-looking customers that the little town saw at any time of the year. The back of many leather vests bore the colors and insignias of different motorcycle clubs. Most of the riders showed off extravagant tattoos. Only three weeks into the fall semester at the nearby college, plenty of new employees worked at the shop, and these newer folks looked a little nervous as they waited on the crowd. But soon they grew at ease as the loud and intimidating-looking group engaged in friendly banter with anyone who would listen to them.

Patrick had known Jimmy as long as he could remember. He and Aunt Mal had gone to school together, and although he only saw Jimmy for a few days each year, Jimmy felt like a part of the family. Jimmy was like that—he had a way of quickly forming connections that left lasting impressions. Although he looked rough around the edges during this weekend visit, Patrick knew better. Jimmy was a radiologist in one of the largest hospitals in Virginia. He was also passionate about riding and the people with which he shared his passion. Every year, he and a number of others made a trip they had come to call the Carolina Coastal Cruise—riding the full length of the North Carolina coast and concluding with a weekend in Aunt Mal's hometown—with much of the time spent at The Lion's Den.

Patrick watched Jimmy throughout the day as the grizzled biker made a point of talking to each and every rider and every employee from The Lion's Den. Some former employees whom Patrick hadn't seen for years showed up that day just to reconnect with Jimmy.

Later that evening, as the band for the afternoon broke down and the evening band began to set up, Jimmy got up and took the microphone. Each year they turned the ride into a benefit to help someone in need. This year they dedicated it to help a rider and his family. He had had a stroke earlier that year, and the family was having difficulty making ends meet. They had raised money through raffle tickets, a silent auction, and sponsor donations. Several others helped Jimmy run the various parts of the program. It culminated with announcing the winner of the 50/50 raffle, where 50 percent of the winnings went to the fundraiser and 50 percent went to the winner. As was customary, the winner donated all of his winnings back to the benefit. The loud group joked and laughed through the entire hour. Then Jimmy got up to announce the total amount raised and to give a little speech.

"This money will make life a little easier for our brother and his family," Jimmy concluded his talk. "But a lot of you have already donated a lot—not just money but time. Many of you were by his bedside, others made meals, and the list goes on and on. This is who we are. We take care of our brothers and sisters." When Jimmy announced the total financial contribution, there was a collective gasp. "That's more than three times what I was expecting. I can't tell you how proud I am to be a part of this group made up of people from so many different motorcycle clubs and walks of life."

The amount itself wasn't as surprising as what Patrick saw all around him in this little coffee shop that had temporarily been transformed into a biker bar. This group of riders that loved being in the wind on their loud bikes, that laughed with a freedom he rarely saw, and that sometimes frightened those who didn't know them...suddenly grew quiet. Tears streamed down the cheeks of many of them. The moment passed quickly, but for the rest of the evening, he saw the group connecting on a deeper level, slapping backs, exchanging words, and sometimes exchanging hugs.

Later in the evening, as the band wound down to the last few songs and the crowd dwindled to the last few stragglers, Aunt Mal approached Patrick. "Come sit with us, Patrick," she said. She had sat chatting with Jimmy for the last few hours. She told Jimmy that Patrick wanted to learn more about LUCK, and as one of the best connectors she knew, she was hoping that Jimmy would teach him what it meant to connect.

"Glad to do what I can," Jimmy smiled, his voice deep and patient.

"There's really not a big secret to it, Patrick. I just do a few things consistently. I start each day with a prayer for those I met the day before, and I end each day with a journal, writing the names of those I met and a few things about each of them." Jimmy went on to describe some tactics he had discovered for getting introduced, remembering names, and starting conversations. Jimmy's appearance and sometimes rough demeanor didn't always make him feel approachable to those who had not yet met him, but Patrick learned that Jimmy followed a process for building relationships that worked.

"The heart of it isn't how I connect, it's why I connect," Jimmy continued. "I connect to serve. My goal is to find out some small way I can help or serve the person I'm talking to and then to follow through. Most of the time what someone needs, is a way to connect with someone else—just like your aunt here connected you to me—and that doesn't take much effort. When I need help with something, like help setting up this ride and the fundraiser, I don't hesitate to ask because I know a lot of other people who take the same approach to relationships.

"Which leads to another thing I try to do. As I connect and build relationships, I try to understand the attitude of others. There are those who are mostly in it for themselves—to get what they can. Then there are those who are mostly in it for others—to give. The givers tend to put energy into relationships. They are positive. And the getters tend to take it out. They are negative. And there are those who are in between. The more positive people one is connected to, the more positive he or she is likely to become, but the inverse is also true. I'm not talking about introverts and extroverts here. I'm not talking about people who are polite and people who are gruff. There are plenty of nice people who will take everything they can. And there are plenty of tough people and introverts who would give you the shirt off of their backs. It takes time to know the difference.

"I've also found that we need to connect on two levels. Connecting with those we know well enables us to go further faster. Connecting with those we have less in common with permanently expands our horizons and opportunities. Both types of connections are important.

"People who you have a lot in common with can't teach you much...do you see that guy?" Jimmy pointed to another rider standing near the band. The man had been one of the loudest of the group since he arrived, and even now he was animated—waving his hands furiously, an irresistible grin on his face while telling some story to the circle of riders gathered around him who occasionally broke out in laughter. "That's Crazy Joe. The guy is a people magnet—everyone wants to be around him. He has a way of inviting everybody into his circle. I wish I could be as natural at creating connections as Joe is. But they call him Crazy because of his hot temper. He's wrecked three bikes at different times when his temper flared. He needed to get that under control or he was headed for trouble.

"About eight years ago, I introduced him to Gunny." Now Jimmy pointed to another individual sitting at the bar. Gunny was older, had a military haircut, solid gray hair, and a powerful build. He sat drinking a beer and chatting with a few others at the bar. "Gunny doesn't need to be in the limelight. He served in Vietnam and has carried the complications of a severe battle injury every day since he came back. He lives in constant pain and can't ride the two wheelers he loves anymore—so he rides a trike. He has plenty of reasons to be negative, but he chooses to be positive. His experiences in life and his temperament couldn't be further from Crazy Joe's.

"Now, all these years later, Crazy Joe isn't the same guy he used to be. Gunny's patience and positive influence has taught him things he didn't realize he didn't know. Gunny, in turn, is connected to a lot more people because of Joe's magnetic personality. Their bond made this entire group better—Joe is like the front door to this group. Whenever a new person is around, Joe makes it a point to make them feel a part of things. Bringing two people with relatively little in common together made both better; it's not what most people intuitively think will work.

"But with those who are extremely negative—who drain all they can from others—I've learned to spot them and keep my distance," Jimmy lowered his voice and locked eyes with Patrick. "Those folks prey on two types of people: those who don't know them and can be fooled for a little while and those who are naïve and will never learn. They can be tough to identify though—they've learned how to play the game and to fool a lot of people, sometimes even themselves. I'm cordial to them but I spend very little time with them." These final words shared by Jimmy that night took years for Patrick to process. Like his mother, Patrick always wanted to believe the best about everyone, and learning to raise his guard with some people was a difficult lesson.

The next morning, they were all saying good-bye after breakfast. Bikers embraced Lauren, Aunt Mal, and even Patrick as they prepared to head back to Virginia. Jimmy walked over to Patrick and said, "Remember three things, kid. First, it's a process, and it's different for everyone. Figure out what it is for you. Second, positive connectors create positive connectors. Connect with the purpose of serving, and help those who are on the cusp become more positive by making the right connections. And third, try to find ways to connect with people who you have weak connections with. Big gains will come from there. The rest will fall into place."

Field Trip

"Sir...sir...can I take your order, sir?" The voice of the cashier snapped him back into the present.

Patrick knew it was time for another field trip. The CEO had mentioned to him a conversation between herself and the COO of their largest distributor. She was surprised to find the distributor had progressed far beyond their company in developing processes for creating connections with customers and employees. She had told Patrick that there were some things that the distributor implemented that sounded like they went against The LUCK Principle, and these tactics appeared to be working well. Above all, however, she had been impressed with the processes that the distributor had put into place for customer relationships and employee collaboration. Patrick's commitment remained rooted in getting to the truth, even if that meant finding out LUCK didn't work in all cases. He invited the distributor to come to their offices and convinced three key members of the executive team, including the CEO, to join them.

As they settled into the meeting, Patrick turned to the COO of the distributor and opened the conversation. "Mr. Taylor, you made quite an impression on our CEO when you discussed how you engage with customers and employees. Can you start by giving us a brief overview of your process for doing that?"

"First of all, please call me Ian," he started. "And which process are you asking about? We have hundreds of processes for relationships. We have processes for our consumer customers, our business customers, and for our large, named accounts. We have brainstorming, lessons-learned, training, coaching, and mentoring processes. We have processes for evaluating the strength and quality of connections between employees and customers. We have web-sales, social-engagement, direct-mail, and influencer processes. We have a loyalty process and program. And we have a governance process, which we developed for the purpose of developing and monitoring our many different relationship processes."

There followed a few moments of silence. Patrick felt overwhelmed at the thought of all these processes, and he knew the others from the company had to be feeling the same thing. On top of that, he was the most junior person in the room, and taking the leadership position proved more than a little bit intimidating.

Patrick finally broke the uncomfortable silence. "You described a specific sales process our CEO felt turned LUCK upside down. In fact, she thought it sounded more like 'CLUCK' because you started with attempting to connect rather than with listening. Maybe you can describe that process," he said glancing at the others. He noticed a few raised eyebrows. He had been preaching LUCK for a while, and he knew it would be a shock to admit that it may not be a silver bullet. But risking transparency was part of what LUCK called for in relationships, and Patrick trusted this group.

Ian quickly broke the tension by laughing loudly and slapping the table. "CLUCK. I like that, Patrick," he said. "The process you're talking about is our account-assessment process, and after thinking about it, I believe it fits very well with your LUCK Principle. We had only just launched the process when I met with your CEO. Even now we're only just starting to see the results, but we're confident it will work well for us and for our prospects."

He then went on to describe a process for reviewing their existing direct-sales accounts. It began with internal research into their purchasing patterns. The next step involved developing a custom presentation for the customer. After this, a meeting with the customer executives followed to show them how they could save time and money and improve quality by altering how they worked together. If all went well, they then engaged in delving deeper with the customer to further analyze the situations and put new processes in place, which ultimately improved business for their customers while also expanding their relationships with them.

"I can see how you felt this sounded like 'CLUCK,'" Ian said, turning toward the CEO. "On the surface, it appears we start by talking to a customer rather than listening. But in reality, we invest significant time in listening before the meeting. We've found what we have to present in these meetings often develops into something very different than what a client would say they're interested in, that it's important we take a lot of control of the conversation at this point. That's the only way we will deliver the kind of valuable service that they wouldn't even know to request.

"But this is just one process," Ian continued. "What took us a long time to learn is that relationship processes develop very differently from other business processes. They remain rigid at the core but flexible around the edges. Think of it as a wheel that has to bear the weight of the full car but also needs to provide durability, flexibility, stability, and agility." Ian drew a circle with spokes on his legal pad as he spoke. "When we tried to model relationship processes after our other business processes, they turned out overly rigid. It felt like driving a car with wheels but no tires—sparks flew. At the other extreme, we would give our team good information with no processes at all, and we had no way to scale or improve—the car veered out of control.

"It's hard to bring rigid-thinking people, like those in technology and accounting, together with flexible-thinking people, like those in sales, marketing and human resources. Heck, it took about four thousand years after the wheel was invented before we added a tire! But that's what relationship processes require.

"Effective customer and employee engagement processes are like a wheel. They are rigid at the core and flexible at the edges. And they have 'RIMS'—they are repeatable, improvable, measurable, and scalable," he concluded, immediately transitioning into another topic.

"We have found that people—customers and employees—have a positive, negative, or neutral effect on connecting. We call those with a positive impact 'stars'—they tend to give energy to others, light them up, and people even come into orbit around their influence. We call those with a negative impact 'black holes'—they tend to suck the energy from those around them. So we have processes in place to try to connect stars to more people—to convert neutral connectors to stars and to convert black holes into neutral agents. But in some cases, we also have to remove some of the black holes entirely.

"Another interesting area we focus on, particularly internally, is the importance of both strong and weak ties. Some of our employees have strong ties with one another, and in those cases, we've found that there is a tremendous amount of overlap of knowledge and experience. When something needs to get done quickly or routinely, these strong ties are helpful. Employees who have weaker ties to one another, however, have more to offer in terms of expanding knowledge and making connections to others. We often bring in outsiders to expand our team—some for projects and some in long-term advisory roles—to be sure we're always introducing fresh perspectives. By creating, or strengthening, weak ties, we create more engagement and innovation.

"And all of this fits very well with your LUCK Principle. In fact, our whole team has embraced your LUCK Principle," Ian concluded, looking directly at Patrick and shifting the attention of everyone in the room to him. "We've discussed it internally and have come to realize it is a great framework for our customer and employee engagement processes. We're going through all of these processes I have mentioned, and continuing to use LUCK to evaluate and improve them. We're relying on it as our guideline for developing new processes. You have one tremendous advantage over where we were when we started, Patrick—you are starting with an excellent framework. We kept trying to build connections without a frame-work, and it held us back for years."

Journal Entry

CONNECT

LEADERSHIP IS THE DRIVER - PROCESS IS THE WHEEL - TECHNOLOGY IS THE ENGINE.

PROCESS MUST BE BALANCED...

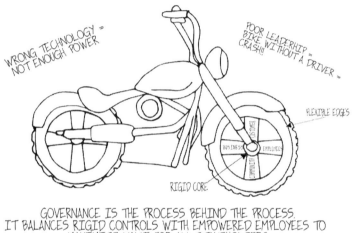

WRONG TECHNOLOGY = NOT ENOUGH POWER

POOR LEADERSHIP = BIKE WITHOUT A DRIVER = CRASH!!

FLEXIBLE EDGES

BUSINESS   EMPLOYEES   COMMUNITY   STAKEHOLDERS

RIGID CORE

GOVERNANCE IS THE PROCESS BEHIND THE PROCESS.
IT BALANCES RIGID CONTROLS WITH EMPOWERED EMPLOYEES TO
MAXIMIZE VALUE FOR ALL STAKEHOLDERS

TOO FLEXIBLE	FLEXIBLE EDGES	RIGID CORE	TOO RIGID
	PRINCIPLES	POLICIES	
	DISCOVERY	CONTROL	
	UNSTRUCTURED	STRUCTURE	
	CONTENT	DATA	
	LEARNING	SCALABILITY	
	TRADITIONS	KPIS AND SOPS	
	EMPOWERMENT	PRODUCTIVITY	
BUSINESS HAS	COLLABORATION	AUTOMATION	
NO CONTROL AND	PERSONALIZATION	CONSISTENCY	UNNECESSARY FRICTION
RUNS OFF THE ROAD			WITH EMPLOYEES
			AND CUSTOMERS

What's the Application?

The CEO put her hand on Patrick's shoulder on the way out of the meeting. "You've got a lot of work to do." She smiled. "I'll expect to be meeting with you monthly for a while to check the status of this LUCK project of yours."

As Patrick thought through all he had heard, he realized that the missing links in his organization were exactly what Jimmy and Ian had pointed out. They had built the tools, and they had the technology to scale relationship processes. But their processes were either entirely missing or were too rigid. As he recalled Ian's example of the wheels on a car, Patrick envisioned his organization as a car with no driver. Their leadership team didn't know how to create these new types of processes. As a result, the engine created more problems than it solved.

The first area Patrick and the CEO focused on involved addressing how they built teams that tackled the challenges of creating relationship processes. In some cases, fast progress was important, so they built teams of individuals who already had strong ties so they could move forward quickly. But much of what they were working on was new to the organization, so in those cases, they pulled diverse teams together to expand on the insights available to the team—often finding outsiders to advise or even lead those teams and bring in fresh perspectives.

They also developed processes and analytical approaches to identify the positive and negative connectors within the organization. They brought together their most positive contributors and teams with those who were having trouble making a contribution and tracked the changes. They saw considerable improvement but still had to go through the painful process of releasing the individuals who didn't belong on the team.

Patrick began to work across the organization to develop processes to improve how teams managed relationships inside and outside of the organization. He established governance processes to engage the leadership team. This included a cadence of meetings, set priorities, and an approach to process development that embraced both rigidity and flexibility. Together, they developed processes to improve the customer experience and unify their workforce, which was now distributed around the globe.

A strategy that took a lot of convincing to get the CEO on board involved the amount of training and coaching required to change how people worked. Patrick had become frustrated with himself with how naïve he had been earlier in this area. He knew from his experience at The Lion's Den that preparing people to be good baristas took weeks of training, mentoring, and reinforcement. He should have known that in their much larger and more complex environment, small changes could take place quickly, but permanently changing the behavior of his team to practice the philosophy, processes, and technologies of LUCK would come incrementally, with continuous training, coaching leaders, and persistent reinforcement—it was more like committing to a fitness program than buying a fitness tracker.

It dawned on Patrick that the only real difference between most businesses was in the human factor—how people creatively interacted with one another. Everything else in the business was gradually becoming automated. Delivering the human factor meant almost constant learning for everyone involved. The ability to innovate and connect could never be automated and was never the same from one organization to the next.

Patrick was gaining greater confidence that the LUCK process could, indeed, be scaled from working with individual relationships to working in a complex business. Lack of success with forming connections, however, gave rise to a new problem. Unbeknownst to Patrick, only a small portion of the significant amount of time he invested into developing processes for connecting would bear fruit. This would change when he uncovered the problem, and unlocked the solution, in something that they were doing every day.

CHAPTER 4
KNOW

*I've not failed. I've just found 10,000
ways that won't work.*
—THOMAS A. EDISON

*Excellent firms don't believe in excellence—only
in constant improvement and constant change.*
—TOM PETERS

*Businesses always have problems. Numbers tell you
where the problems are, and how worried you should be.*
—JACK STACK

*Remember, we don't want to think about
profits first, but we do want to be sure someone
is thinking about them at some point.*
—KEN GOLDSTEIN

*When you're dealing with big business,
it's easy to forget that you're dealing with
people and that people have feelings. It's easy
to just look at it like a business unit.*
—KELLY RIPA

Introduction

"LUCK feels like a New Year's resolution to me," the CFO, Brandt Reeb, deadpanned. "We may know it's the right thing to do, and we may have started strong. But we've fizzled out. I know it can transform this business, but if we can't find the self-discipline to stick with it, then it's a serious waste of time and money."

Patrick had recently celebrated his fourteen-year work anniversary and shortly thereafter accepted a promotion to the role of executive vice president of sales, marketing, and service. He had come further than he had ever expected to and risen to be a part of the leadership team faster than any employee before him. He had applied The LUCK Principle throughout the journey, had trained others in it, and had used it to manage his teams. A few years earlier, he had convinced the leadership team that the principle should be applied across the entire company. But as he sat in the boardroom with his boss, Brandt, and five of his peers, he felt more like a rookie intern than a seasoned business executive with a proven approach for engaging customers and employees.

Brandt meant to overstate his case, Patrick knew. Over the years, they had put some amazing systems and processes in place with undeniable impact. Individuals connected, innovated, and improved how the company did business more effectively than before. They helped expand the company more efficiently than they had just five years ago. But many of the processes the organization had put into place, including many managed by Patrick's team, had fizzled out, as Brandt had said, because of lack of follow-through.

Evidence in reports clearly showed that the processes, when followed, made a tremendous difference, making their failure even more frustrating for Patrick. People kept falling back into old habits, gut-level decisions, and ad-hoc approaches rather than sticking with the processes. Patrick had worked with his team to measure results religiously as part of the "know" part of LUCK.

What could he have missed? How was a little coffee shop able to have more self-discipline than a business hundreds of times larger? He reviewed what he thought he knew as he stepped on the elevator to return to his office.

Infographic

Organizations where employees know the score, how they contribute to it, and are invited to participate in improving and innovating, outperform their peers.

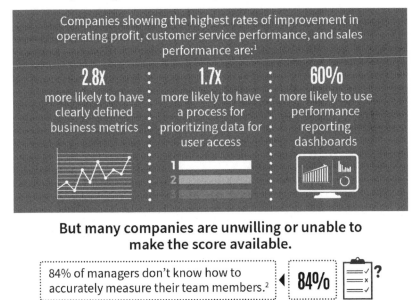

Companies showing the highest rates of improvement in operating profit, customer service performance, and sales performance are:[1]

2.8x : **1.7x** : **60%**

more likely to have clearly defined business metrics : more likely to have a process for prioritizing data for user access : more likely to use performance reporting dashboards

But many companies are unwilling or unable to make the score available.

84% of managers don't know how to accurately measure their team members.[2] ◀ **84%** ?

And most fail to engage the full team in the process.

79% GAP

▶ **86%** 86% of leaders say that it is critical to collaborate across boundaries.[3]

▶ **7%** Only 7% felt that they were highly effective at doing so.[3]

The ingredients for continuous improvement and innovation?
• Understand and share the score at the corporate, team and individual level.
• Analyze failure and celebrate success together.
• Build transparency and vulnerability into the process.

Download the full Infographic at: www.theLUCKprinciple.com/gotBook

In The Lion's Den

"Boom!" Patrick exclaimed as he dropped his first semester report card on the coffee shop bar.

He beamed with pride. "Straight A's! I made the dean's list!" It was a cool afternoon, just before Christmas, and the coffee shop was almost empty during this quiet time of year, with few students or tourists in town.

"This is great, sweetie. Really, just excellent," said Lauren as she picked up the slip of paper and looked at it. "But I bet you can do even better."

Patrick was stunned. He felt like an inflated balloon that had been released before someone tied a knot in the stem.

"How…How's that even possible? This is perfect." He stammered the words out. "That's not fair," was the unspoken sentiment in his voice.

Lauren spoke in an intentional and calm tone, draining as much emotion as she could from what she said. "Are you going to school and working so hard just so you can get a slip of paper with some little letters on it?" she started. "Or is there something more?" She registered Patrick's confusion and tried a new course. "Let me put it another way. Is life about having a pulse? Or is there something more to it? Is a business more than about making a profit? All of these things are important—to survive you need them—but those things aren't really what life, school, or business are all about."

"What is that?" Patrick muttered, not really interested in the conversation after having his bubble burst. "What measure of success is more important than grades or profits?"

"In a word: failure," Lauren said plainly. "This is a great report card; it should be celebrated. We will celebrate it together. You think you know you are successful based on these grades. But really knowing if we are successful is much deeper. Even in our greatest success, failure dwells. A gap exists between every one of us and perfection. To practice the principle of 'Know,' you need to see the gap and always work on narrowing it. Ask yourself—why are good grades in school so important to you?"

He paused as he considered his answer. Then Patrick, for the first time, told his mother about his decision to work on scaling LUCK to work in businesses. Engineering and developing products that millions of people would benefit from had long been his passion, and now he had added LUCK to that. He would start with engineering, but he now envisioned a career focused on applying The LUCK Principle in business to benefit thousands of employee and customer relationships.

Now it was Lauren's turn to be stunned. She sat in silence for a few moments as a range of emotions played out on her face. Confusion was quickly followed by understanding, then pride, and then tearful joy.

"So," she started. Her eyes reddened and she spoke in a hoarse whisper that she could never control when she was choking back tears of happiness, "Ask yourself—in addition to getting into the university, getting great grades, and then getting a good job, what is *really* needed?"

Patrick sat in awkward silence, partly because he couldn't think of an answer and partly because he never knew how to handle his mother when she got this way.

"You told me that in some of your group projects, you had some teammates who wouldn't work hard or who just didn't get it. So you worked doubly hard to make up for them. You weren't going to let their weaknesses keep you from achieving your goals. But what would it look like if you learned how to practice LUCK with them so they worked harder to get the job done? What would it look like if you helped them to contribute to the success of the team?"

"Well...sounds nice," Patrick considered. "But also risky. Might mean even more work, and I might not get an A if I trusted them so blindly."

"Yes, that's true," Lauren said. "But even if it's harder work and even if you don't get an A, I think you would have gained much more than you would have only by getting the A. Even if your mission were just to be a great employee someday, learning how to practice LUCK to help others to make their best possible contribution is at least as important as the grade itself. For the mission you have chosen, it's even more important that you learn how to engage with others to get results.

"Knowing means knowing the score everyone sees—the grade or the profit," Lauren continued, "but that's really only like knowing you have a pulse. Yes, it's very important—without it nothing else matters. But knowing also requires digging deeper. You have to become aware, even in success, that there is always some failure—everything can always be improved."

"But isn't that kind of negative?" Patrick asked, still chafing from getting no "Atta boy" for his report card.

"It's true," Aunt Mal interjected after having listened in on the conversation as long as she could silently. "We're imperfect people. Even in our very best accomplishments, there is a better way we missed. Think about history—many of the people who helped us make strides forward in science, freedom, medicine, and human rights would be considered unenlightened by today's standards—maybe they did as well as they could, given the times they lived in, but more could always have been done. It's our job to always try to know the results and how they can be improved so that the gap shrinks. Sometimes the better way is a small improvement, and sometimes it is a disruptive innovation.

"When you see the truth about failure, you remain humble and vulnerable. You listen to others for ways to improve. If you don't see the truth in this, you find yourself growing arrogant, and you defensively resist change and become closed to the thinking of others. I know to a young pup like you, this seems a little silly—but your philosophy drives your attitude, your attitude drives your actions, and your actions drive results. Nothing is more important. Do you want to transform from a caterpillar into a butterfly? Then you need to be prepared to spend some time in an ugly, vulnerable cocoon!" Having finished her speech, Aunt Mal reached across the bar, cupped her hands over Patrick's ears, pulled him forward, and kissed him on top of his head. "Here endeth the lesson," she said with a wink.

Lauren had a broad grin as she started again. "Honey, you're right. It was negative to start with failure. It really wasn't fair for me to go straight there after you showed me this wonderful report card. Celebrating hard work and success is important too, and that's where you should start. But when the time comes, you also have to open yourself up, become vulnerable, and have others you trust help you identify your failures. Never wallow in it—move on quickly." She hesitated for a few moments, then asked, "Do you know how many businesses I've started?"

"Three?" Patrick answered, thinking of the coffee shop and a couple of others that she partly owned.

"Twelve. Nine failed," she said with an unusual show of pride. "I learned more from each of the nine failures than I have from all three of the successes combined. Everything I do is better for what I have learned from failure."

"You probably think I named this place The Lion's Den because I like lions. I really named it that because what I needed to learn to run this shop was forged through many painful experiences. I felt like I'd gone through a lion's den a few times before I was able to create something that survived. Failure is not weakness. Not trying, not taking any risks, or not owning our failures—that's weakness. The Lion's Den is where we come to know our failures, we learn, and we move on. Those few brave souls who have failed but learned, who have faced down the lion and risen again—those are the strong."

"But *how* do you keep score?" asked Patrick. "What is there besides grades to help me know?"

"I do it in a lot of ways. The most important thing I do is meditate and connect to my creator—when I compare myself to perfection, I always strive for more, and it keeps me from becoming arrogant. I also keep a journal, as you know. I have a vision for where I want to go, goals and plans. I also review and refine all of them regularly. Other things I track on my report card—goals I have achieved and people I've helped. But one of the most important and difficult ways I keep score is by asking people."

"Why is it difficult?" Patrick asked.

"Because it is extremely rare to find people who know you well enough to see the problems. Rarer still to find people who will tell you the truth. But the most difficult challenge is not *finding* the right person, it is *being* the right person. You must become the kind of person that others feel safe approaching to talk about your failures.

"To get started, focus on this most difficult thing—become a person who can be vulnerable. Trust a small circle of others to open yourself up. Risk letting a few in so they can see where you fail. You'll have to trust them to not hurt you with that knowledge. Sometimes I've trusted the wrong people, and so will you, but you don't stop trying. Making yourself vulnerable to a few people is an absolute must if you're going to be successful at failure."

Field Trip

Patrick had carefully incorporated what he had learned about the "Know" principle into his organization. Team leaders kept score and measured the standard financials. Together they tracked key performance indicators and qualitative lessons learned that they discussed as a team. He had worked on modeling vulnerability and fusing this into his team so that team members would have a safe place to learn from their failures.

Still, they were missing something. People were not as engaged as he knew they could be, and as a result, they lost focus. They failed to adopt changes and new processes or develop new innovations as fast as he knew they could. He had lost something in trying to scale what he had learned about the "Know" principle in the coffee shop to a global business.

As he headed toward his office, his phone dinged to remind him of a meeting he had arranged with the chief information officer of a nearby company to learn how it measured its business results. Forty-five minutes later, Patrick and the information technology director for his company, Anne-Mari, sat in a conference room across town on another field trip. Patrick and Anne-Mari had practically become joined at the hip over the last five years as The LUCK Principle took hold, and they worked closely on making it more scalable across their growing organization.

Patrick began the meeting by explaining The LUCK Principle and the struggles they had experienced developing new innovations and creating sustainable change at the desired pace.

"You are stuck where we were about three years ago," Jay started. "Your ideas on keeping score more efficiently, sharing the numbers with the team, educating your people on how to understand the numbers, giving them a voice to have an impact, and a safe environment to analyze failure all hit the mark. In fact, we've gone through the painful process of discovering that if someone doesn't need to know the score to do their job, then they're not really on the team.

"Great organizations are great at failure. Vulnerability is a prerequisite for becoming great at failure. Building those into your culture is a great start.

"But you're still missing a subtle but critical ingredient." He paused and looked at each of them for dramatic effect. "Meetings," he declared after a moment.

Patrick had to clench his teeth to keep his jaw from dropping open. One thing he was sure they didn't need to add to the program was more meetings. They had meetings on top of meetings. In fact, he was trying to find ways to schedule fewer meetings. More time-wasting meetings? Patrick knew this must have shocked Anne-Mari as much as it did him.

Jay smiled as if he could read their minds.

"Our epiphany came when we looked at our teams. Most of them were getting humdrum results. But one team was killing it. Top- and bottom-line contributions were off the charts for this team compared to the other teams. The improvements and innovations to sales, product development, technology, and other areas that this team developed stuck; it could change and adopt new processes on an entirely different scale than the other teams."

Now Patrick leaned forward in his chair.

"Everything that team did looked the same on paper. But when we started cross-training other teams by sending them to those meetings, we realized the type and structure of the meetings made the difference. The team had a disciplined schedule of standard meetings on a weekly, monthly, quarterly, and annual cycle. These enabled everyone to have input across everything from annual planning to daily tasks. So everyone on the team was producing insights on improvement and innovation, and because they remained engaged in the process, they bought into these changes. The regular meetings focused on institutionalizing the changes, thus the changes stuck and produced lasting results. When we made this discovery and scaled it across the company, we then discovered that more innovation is produced from lateral collaboration compared with either top-down or bottom-up planning. That changed everything.

"We also stopped meeting to talk about systems, procedures, and numbers. Our meetings are now almost entirely focused on customers. We exist to serve customers, and we want to improve how we engage with them—the numbers tell us how we're doing in that effort, and the systems and procedures are our tools for delivery. But we exist to satisfy the customer. When we help employees engage with one another about engaging with customers, it creates ownership and not just 'buy in.' Employees who *build* a process thrive on owning and improving it; employees who are *assigned* a process tolerate implementing it. People want to be part of a bigger picture, and the bigger picture is always the customer."

Jay, Anne-Mari, and Patrick spent the next forty-five minutes talking in detail about how to create a meeting structure and other collaboration tools and approaches to foster lateral collaboration. Patrick felt confident that, when combined with what they were already doing, this would help them master the process of not only knowing their results but also continuously improving and innovating at a fast pace.

As their time drew to a close, Anne-Mari brought up a different subject. "Jay," she started, "the reason Patrick asked me to join this meeting is we expected a part of what we were missing to be technology. But I'm surprised you've barely mentioned it—particularly since you're the CIO. What part has technology played in this process?"

"Technology had almost nothing to do with solving our problems," Jay responded without hesitation, "but it proved critical for scaling the solutions. In fact, now that I think about it, technology created more problems than it solved. Once we have a solution to a problem, technology makes us efficient at executing it. When we were in your position, Anne-Mari, we were asking the same question you just asked. We rummaged for a quick fix. We threw all sorts of software, apps, and technology at the problem, and it solved nothing. For the most part, our people didn't want and didn't use the technology—they often complained it only slowed them down.

"But once we solved our people and process problems, our teams started clamoring for the right technologies so they could work together better to scale the pace of productivity, innovation, and improvement. That's when we started effectively using technology to increase the pace of change. We use customer relationship management applications to capture and share customer information and automate many processes. Collaboration applications revolutionized how we share ideas and information internally, how we work together across offices, how our leadership team listens to front-line employees, and how people find what they're looking for quickly to get their jobs done. Big-data applications have enabled us to share numbers in real time, so we can always know the score on how we are doing everywhere in the business. We often evaluate new technologies and pilot them—and sometimes those technologies have played an important role in changing how we think about a problem—but this is always done within the context of brainstorming how the technology can be used to help us make the customer experience better.

"Technology can either de-humanize or super-humanize the workplace. When we focused primarily on technology, not much changed. We scheduled meetings to plan the technology, meetings to use the technology, meetings to try to improve adoption of the technology. Eventually, when we stopped meeting to talk about technology and started meeting to engage employees in conversations about the business and about engaging customers, things began to slowly change for the better. Emphasis on slowly.

"Most businesses are addicted to the quick-fix mentality. We realized quick fixes just pave potholes. We didn't want to pave the potholes; we wanted a new highway. Building a new highway means careful planning, a lot of construction, and many delays while new traffic patterns are established.

"We wanted to transform into a great organization, constantly narrowing the gap between the present and the perfect. Transformation of that type is never a quick fix."

Journal Entry

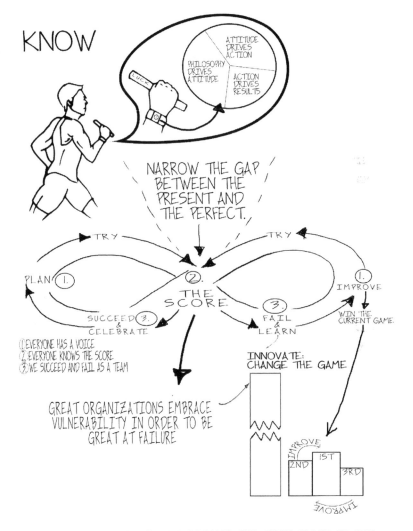

IF SOMEONE DOESN'T NEED TO KNOW THE SCORE, THEN THEY'RE NOT ON THE TEAM

What's the Application?

"We have a great culture here, where people feel safe being vulnerable talking about how we have failed," Anne-Mari observed during the ride back home. "That's rare. In fact, that might be the hardest part of continually improving. But we need learn to leverage that strength to engage the entire team in the process of innovation and improvement."

"We've made a lot of progress in sharing the numbers with the team," Patrick noted, "and although that took a lot of hard work, it may have been the easy part. We need to do a better job of helping everyone understand what the numbers mean and, maybe a more difficult task still, creating a structure where we give everyone a voice. Business is a team sport, but folks can't contribute to a team if they don't know the score or their roles in improving the score."

"I must confess," Anne-Mari responded thoughtfully, "that I've often invested in technology without really understanding that the purpose of all technology investments is to improve the customer experience and how we collaborate in that process." Anne-Mari paused as Patrick nodded.

"But," Anne-Mari added somewhat hesitantly, "I think you've made the same mistake with employee engagement sometimes." She paused to let that sink in, and then went on. "The purpose of employee engagement is to create a better customer experience—not to create a better employee experience. But when employees engage in such an effort, they benefit too. It's human nature—when one side of the relationship equation is happy, the other side tends to reciprocate."

Patrick took a moment to think this over and expressed agreement with Anne-Mari's assessment.

Then she smiled. "You know, Patrick, we're doing exactly what we want the entire company to do. We're working together to improve the process of how we should be working together to follow and improve the process!"

They both enjoyed a laugh at the irony of their discussion and continued to strategize on how they could apply what they had learned.

They introduced their departments to a new approach to collaboration based on improving customer engagement. After some success with their own teams, they convinced the leadership team to restructure how the entire organization engaged.

Interestingly enough, Brandt Reeb, the CFO, was the toughest to convince. Once they had convinced him, however, they enlisted his support to start making more numbers available and to educate each team on how to interpret and understand them. Thus they discovered that transparency with company numbers drives employee engagement, engenders enhanced customer experiences, and fosters innovation.

Patrick and Anne-Mari also agreed to stop doing one thing that had become a habit: They would no longer talk about how to convince teams to adopt technology. After their discussion with Jay, they had come to realize that it was never just about technology. It had always been about improving the business and the productivity of the team. Technology played an important role, but it was just a means to that end. Talking about adopting technology almost always means missing the bigger picture of exceeding customer expectations and improving the organization.

Jay pegged it when he said it wasn't a quick fix. They made significant progress in the first year, but it took several years before they felt that the right habits had been learned and institutionalized. By then, they had not only fine-tuned the process but had also applied technology to bring it to scale. All the while, they had to consistently share the numbers, make the business a safe place to learn from failure, educate employees, and create a structure for top-down, bottom-up, and lateral planning, evaluation, innovation, and improvement.

Patrick's journal grew, full of ideas and lessons learned, and he thought how much faster he could scale LUCK if he were starting over with all of this knowledge. Now, well into his career, he was thrilled with the results, but he was surprised at how long and how much work it had taken to get LUCK into every corner of the business.

When his CEO walked into his office to ask him to help another troubled company, he was about to find out just how easy the process had been for his company. The CEO presented Patrick with the biggest challenge of his life.

CHAPTER 5
GOOD LUCK

The biggest difference between givers who succeed and givers who fail is asking for help.
—ADAM M. GRANT

Remember teamwork begins by building trust. And the only way to do that is to overcome our need for invulnerability.
—PATRICK LENCIONI

If you don't have a really clear vision of where you're going, it's almost impossible to get there.
—BO BURLINGHAM

The two most important days in your life are the day you are born and the day you find out why.
—MARK TWAIN

Love your neighbor as yourself.
—JESUS

Introduction

Blind luck.

Patrick had never thought his mother's concept of "Good LUCK"—the fifth and final part of The LUCK Principle—belonged in business. It seemed so deeply personal that scaling it to a large business didn't intuitively make sense to him. But now, as he listened to the story of a failing business, the transformational role that "Good LUCK" plays in business came crashing down as a sudden revelation. Patrick realized blind luck, or what Aunt Mal would say is a blessing, is why he had never had to connect "Good LUCK" to business before. The company he had worked for during his entire career had a foundation of "Good LUCK." Into that fertile ground he had gradually planted seeds. So LUCK was already a deep part of the culture at his company by the time he had begun to focus on scaling it.

Larry's company didn't have the same benefit.

Patrick's CEO asked him to meet with Larry. She and Larry were long-time friends, and she knew his business was struggling. Now, with a reputation as a leader in business thinking, Patrick spent more time helping other businesses apply LUCK, so this request was an exciting challenge for him.

"Larry," Patrick said slowly after having spent many hours with Larry understanding his situation, "I'm afraid I have very bad news for you. Your company is already practicing a lot of LUCK—but it's not what is going to turn your situation around."

Larry's already grim expression seemed permanent. He had grown so used to bad news since replacing Steve, the former CEO, that it hardly phased him anymore. "So that's it, then," he said, more a statement than as a question, "LUCK isn't going to help, and I need to look elsewhere for a fix, if there is one."

"LUCK *alone* won't," Patrick responded, "but I think '*Good* LUCK' can. But you need to understand that it won't be easy, there will be painful decisions—it's not a quick fix."

Larry cautiously raised an eyebrow, betraying a hint of optimism, but his frown didn't disappear. He wasn't daring to get too hopeful until he heard more. "What is '*Good* LUCK'?"

It was the same question Patrick had asked all those years ago, on his last day at the coffee shop before heading off to the university to finish college.

Infographic

Culture starts with leadership character, and directly impacts the bottom line.

(5X)

Character driven leaders and their teams deliver as much as 5x greater returns for their organizations.[1]

50%

The difference in operating profit performance for customer-facing employees that can be explained by culture.[2]

> But having a written mission or values statement, alone, shows no impact on business performance.

▼

Trust, modeled from the top down, is critical to employee engagement.

14%

Only 14 % believe that their company's leaders are ethical and honest.[3]

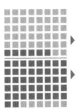

disengaged employees
8%

92%
fully engaged employees

Only 8% of disengaged employees trust their senior management, but 92% of fully engaged employees trust their senior management.[4]

> *Creating a culture of Good LUCK means clearly defined people-centric values, a trusted leadership team that lives out those values, and employees that choose to be contagiously engaged.*

Download the full Infographic at: www.theLUCKprinciple.com/gotBook

In The Lion's Den

It had grown very late that summer Saturday evening, and the three of them were exhausted. A bittersweet feeling hung in the humid North Carolina air, so heavy it was almost as palpable as the ever-present coffee aromas. They worked together one final time to close down the coffee shop. After making sure no one was left in The Lion's Den except for them, Patrick paused in his sweeping, locked the door, and asked the question.

"So…what *is* 'Good LUCK'?"

Lauren's eyes met Patrick's. In spite of the wrinkles that had begun appearing around them a few years ago, her eyes still sparkled. Behind them he could discern a lifetime of wisdom—the kind that isn't learned in a book. She sat down and began to talk. It was clear that she had been thinking about this moment for a long time, but she still struggled to put her thoughts into words.

"'Good LUCK' reminds us that it is just as important to practice LUCK on ourselves as it is to use it to engage with others. This never occurred to me until I realized LUCK was not getting me anywhere. In fact, it seemed to be doing the opposite. It was about eight years after your aunt and I had started the coffee shop. The shop floundered along, making just enough money for us to survive. Yet it consumed me. I worked hard and practiced LUCK with people the best way I knew, but my goals seemed to be slipping ever further away. I couldn't even seem to find the time to do some of the most important things—like spending time with you."

"Your mother is the most selfless and giving person I've ever known," Aunt Mal jumped in. "She practiced LUCK just like she had been taught. But she was giving it all away. There was no room left for her because she didn't know how to practice LUCK on herself."

"You see," Lauren resumed, having collected her thoughts again. "LUCK can be very 'other'-focused. I was giving to everyone self-lessly. But I'd lost sight of what I wanted...what goals I had set and what I was living for...so I was running out of energy. The things I knew I wanted to succeed in—including running this shop—had gone from feeling like a living thing to feeling like a dreadful, decaying burden. I was letting everyone take too much. A few very close to me tried to protect me. Many obliviously took whatever I gave, and a few were knowingly taking advantage of me. So I grew cynical and even a little bitter. I kept thinking if I could just work a little harder and give a little more, then eventually things would work out."

There was a long pause. Clearly she had endured some painful situations during that time. She looked tired and much older as she described it. Patrick had stopped sweeping and leaned on his broom as he listened intently to his mother, as he pushed back a sense of rage that anyone would take advantage of her. Maybe he was biased, but his mother was the most generous soul he had known. She shifted in her chair, sat up a little straighter, and brightened a bit.

"Your Aunt Mal didn't seem to be having the same problem," Lauren continued. "She worked hard in the shop just like I did, and she had her art, surfing, and other community activities, too. In fact, she was one person who took on even more responsibilities for the shop during this time even, although she was so busy already. At some point, I went to her and shared my frustrations. She told me what you've heard her say time and again."

"'The Good Book says to love others as yourself. Not instead of or more than yourself.'" Lauren did a comical impression of Aunt Mal's voice that made both Patrick and Aunt Mal laugh loudly, mostly because it helped to cut the tension in the muggy summer air.

"Put differently," she said, "successful people never forget that people are the most important thing, and that they are one of those people. Some people struggle with remembering other people. Others struggle remembering to take care of their own needs.

"I had a clear picture of what I wanted my life to be," Lauren continued, "what I wanted to accomplish, and how I wanted to give back. But I also had this idea that LUCK was only focused externally, and if I just focused on practicing LUCK on others, it would come back to me. It didn't work that way. LUCK isn't karma. And it wasn't because anyone was doing anything wrong. It was my problem. Things started to turn around when Aunt Mal helped me to practice LUCK on myself—listening to my own voice, connecting to the things important to me, and asking others for help. When I identified my own purpose—my 'Good LUCK'—as a high calling just as important as practicing LUCK on others, things began to get better."

Aunt Mal had pulled a decorative antique scale down from a shelf and set it on the bar. "Maybe this will help," she said. "Most things in life have an opposite. But 'Good LUCK' has two opposites.

"On this side is selfless LUCK." As she said this, she poured coffee beans onto the left side of the scale and it tilted to the left. "If all the weight is on this side, you are being selfless. You burn out and leave yourself open to becoming a doormat. You're not of much use to yourself or anyone else if you let that happen. This is where your mom was stuck.

"On the other side is selfish LUCK." She scooped the beans out of the left side of the scale and poured them into the right side. The scale tilted to that side. "This is when we become manipulative and self-serving. Sure, we may practice LUCK, but it is always with the purpose of fulfilling our own ambitions. A lot of people operate this way—you can tell who they are by who they focus their attention on…only those who can help them attain their goals.

"Bad LUCK is either of those extremes, but 'Good LUCK,'" she scooped half of the beans out of the right side and put them on the left, "balances practicing LUCK on others with practicing it on yourself." The scale slowly tilted until it came into balance. "It can be easy to let the scale tilt to one side or the other—staying in balance takes work."

"OK," said Patrick slowly, "I get that we need to keep things in balance and be neither selfish nor selfless. But how do I practice LUCK on myself?"

"You take the four principles and turn them inward," said Lauren. "You need to listen to yourself. Who are you? What is your purpose? What were you made to do? What are you good at? What gives you a sense of accomplishment? And remember it—keep it in writing and review it regularly. I can't tell you what yours will be, but I can tell you the only purpose with lasting value involves work and involves people. We were made for good work, work that somehow serves others.

"And you need to understand. Why are those things important to you? What is your plan for getting there? What sacrifices will you make? Where should you go to make progress? Are you being true to yourself, or are you chasing someone else's idea?

"Then you need to connect with that. You need to take action. You need to carve out time every week to make sure you are moving in the right direction.

"And you need to constantly evaluate how you are doing so you will know if you are heading in the right direction. Have you made progress? Where have you failed? What have you learned? What new things have you learned about yourself, which require a change in the vision you're moving toward? Are you in balance, or are you tipping the scales too far in one direction or another?

"'Good LUCK' entails balancing the inward and the outward," Aunt Mal summarized. "When focusing on the outward, you build trust as the foundation of relationships. When focusing on the inward, you're true to yourself. By bringing them together, you develop a sense of purpose that serves those around you without losing yourself."

They continued to talk late into the evening about "Good LUCK" and all it meant. Aunt Mal closed the conversation with a comment that would challenge Patrick for the rest of his life: "You have to decide who holds your scales. You can't trust yourself or any person for that job. Who will you trust?"

Practicing "Good LUCK" would be a lifelong exercise for Patrick. But it started late that night after he walked home and wrote in his journal what had been on his mind for a long time: "My purpose: I will learn how to scale LUCK in business, and I will help as many others do this as I possibly can."

Field Trip

Patrick described what he had learned about "Good LUCK" to Larry and then confessed, "Until now, I really didn't have a good idea of how 'Good LUCK' scaled to work in a business. You need to know that I haven't done a lot with it yet."

They discussed the history and situation of Larry's company at length. Larry had started a business, and it had grown over the years. It had been built on many of the principles of LUCK although they didn't call it that. The company was doing well when Larry accepted a buy-out offer from a larger company. It looked like an easy decision at the time, something that would help them grow to the next level and benefit everyone in the organization. But their cultures clashed, and Larry was shocked at how the new leadership treated employees, vendors, and even some of their customers. After a few years, it became clear that the company had plateaued and started to turn downward. When the board fired the CEO, it asked Larry to step in to lead the much larger overall company, and he accepted. It was only once Larry obtained full control of the company that he discovered how bad the situation had grown. That was seven months ago.

"Just two years of bad LUCK has nearly destroyed over twenty years of 'Good LUCK,'" Larry lamented.

As they talked, Patrick reflected on Aunt Mal's scales and how his mother had tilted the scale too far to one side while Larry's company had tilted it too far to the other side. He wondered how many people with good intentions had started businesses to serve others but had gone out of business because they didn't know how to maintain balance.

Over the next two years, Patrick met with Larry regularly. The inner workings of LUCK remained present—in fact, those customer-experience and innovation processes kept the company alive. The deeper issue involved the trust that had been lost between company leadership and the employees. Their once people-centered values had been replaced with a singular focus on profit. These changes had caused some of the best employees to leave, and most of those who remained had disengaged and simply followed rigid processes rather than striving to live up to a set of principles.

Restoring trust was a long road. Larry's return as CEO had some immediate benefit, and even some employees who had departed decided to return under his leadership. But many on the team had never worked with Larry, and it took a long time to convince them that meaningful change had taken place. During this time, Patrick and Larry worked together to engage the whole team in redefining a sense of purpose for the company and developing a plan for modeling trust and purpose from the top down.

It was during one of these meetings that Larry experienced an epiphany. "We follow the 'Know' principle to listen to the pulse of the company, and 'Good LUCK' is about the heart creating that pulse, the reason why people join the company and remain engaged there. Most of them want to belong to something bigger than themselves, something that aligns with their own sense of purpose."

Larry pushed for a mission focused first on the employees in the organization. As admirable as that would be, Patrick pushed back. "Think of a personal mission," Patrick said. "If your own mission is all about yourself, it is narcissistic and hollow. I believe the same is true of a company. A team with a passionate focus on serving a customer, in balance with the needs of employees and the others that they serve, will go much further than a team focused on serving itself. In fact, the more laser-focused you are on providing something valuable for a customer, the more engaged your employees become."

Their values extended beyond just customers and employees. Larry and Patrick made sure to treat every stakeholder—suppliers, vendors, job applicants, shareholders, and the people in the communities in which they operated—with respect. "How we treat the people who have the least to offer in return is the true measure of our character as a company," Larry told his team in a company meeting.

Patrick then spent much of his time coaching Larry and his leadership team on how to live out their mission. This often entailed painful conversations to hold them to it. He knew no mission was worth the paper it was written on. In fact, the previous CEO had defined what appeared to be an admirable mission but never lived up to it. The only meaning in a mission arose from the way the leaders managed themselves. With Larry, Patrick partnered with a leader who understood this and appreciated accountability.

Almost immediately after starting to work together, Patrick and Larry created much more transparency within the company—the "Know" principle. But they sometimes struggled with those decisions. The tough state of the business scared some of their best people off. And it sometimes had a demotivating effect on others who were still having trouble trusting the leadership team.

"Trust is expensive to build, easy to break, and nearly impossible to rebuild," Patrick repeated the words he had heard frequently from Aunt Mal when talking to the leadership team one day. "How people treat you is a reflection of your entire history with them, not just your most recent action. That's why change is so difficult."

Patrick, Larry, and the entire leadership team had to redouble their efforts to communicate and to give people a voice in turning the company around. This process also slowly rebuilt a foundation of trust. The best people in the company began to realize that many other companies lumbered along in the same situation but never trusted their people enough to invite them into the process.

Then there were all of the difficult decisions that only leaders could make. To survive, they would need to eliminate costs and even let go of some good people. To change the culture, they would need to give some people an opportunity to change, and if those employees couldn't do so, then some of them had to be let go. Leaders would have to do it in a way that continued to foster trust, transparency, and vulnerability across the team. This demanded the hardest work that Patrick or Larry performed during the entire project.

"You don't need to worry about my commitment," Larry told Patrick after a particularly long day. "I want this to be a great organization. And great organizations never forget that they only exist to serve their customers and their employees. I'm one of those employees. Everything we do here is either geared toward building or destroying relationships, and relationships are the only real asset that an organization possesses."

But as they slowly rebuilt the company and the relationships, they found that they were gifted with enhanced flexibility. Employees were willing to forego some of the things that they had previously felt entitled to have, suppliers often gave them better pricing and payment terms, the leadership team became invested in a long-term strategy and didn't demand immediate returns, and even their distributors and customers began to offer more flexible terms. The good will generated by fostering trust played an important role in helping them to navigate through the sometimes rocky waters of recovery.

Journal Entry

Good LUCK

LUCK TENDS TO FOCUS ON THE EXTERNAL - SERVING OTHERS.
GOOD LUCK FOCUSES INTERNALLY.

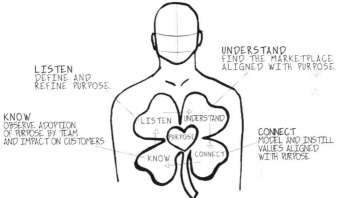

UNDERSTAND
FIND THE MARKETPLACE
ALIGNED WITH PURPOSE.

LISTEN
DEFINE AND
REFINE PURPOSE.

KNOW
OBSERVE ADOPTION
OF PURPOSE BY TEAM
AND IMPACT ON CUSTOMERS

CONNECT
MODEL AND INSTILL
VALUES ALIGNED
WITH PURPOSE

WITHOUT PROFITS OR PAYCHECKS AN ORGANIZATION WILL CEASE TO
EXIST, BUT THOSE ARE NOT REASONS WHY AN ORGRANIZATION EXISTS.

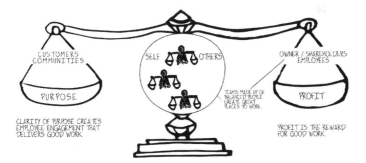

CUSTOMERS
COMMUNITIES

SELF — OTHERS

OWNER / SHAREHOLDERS
EMPLOYEES

PURPOSE

TEAMS MADE UP OF
BALANCED PEOPLE
CREATE GREAT
PLACES TO WORK

PROFIT

CLARITY OF PURPOSE CREATES
EMPLOYEE ENGAGEMENT THAT
DELIVERS GOOD WORK

PROFIT IS THE REWARD
FOR GOOD WORK

GREAT ORGANIZATIONS NEVER FORGET THAT THEY EXIST TO SERVE PEOPLE

What's the Application?

Patrick learned many lessons while working to serve Larry and his company. He brought these lessons back to his own company and to other companies that came to him for help.

He discovered that LUCK is a seed that can scale into a mighty tree, but only if it is planted in the right soil. "Good LUCK" is the soil. Without the balance of "Good LUCK," an organization would almost certainly miss the transformational power of following The LUCK Principle. With it, a team will find the way to LUCK in spite of all obstacles. And as much as he believed in having a written mission, he also found that living a mission was far more important than writing a mission. A team that trusts its leadership and understands where the organization is going will succeed. A well-written mission without authentic leadership will fail.

Keeping balance is a persistent challenge. LUCK points externally, and "Good LUCK" points the same principles inwardly. Profits and paychecks aren't the reasons why a business exists, but without them, a business will cease to exist.

He found it was far easier to fall off a "Good LUCK" foundation than it was to rebuild one. Many good companies fell away from a good foundation. However, few companies were able to get back onto a good foundation once they had fallen off. One of the biggest risks entailed bringing in a large new group of people who didn't follow the same principles. Patrick's company grew steadily, and part of this came from acquiring other companies, so this lesson frightened him more than any of the others. For the other measures he had put into place, he set up special reviews and processes within his company to constantly improve their foundation of "Good LUCK" and to never take it for granted.

Above all, he remembered that "culture" and "brand" existed as a combination of the beliefs and attitudes of everyone who worked in the organization. Sustaining the company's focus on "Good LUCK" wasn't the job of a person or a team—it was the job of every person in the organization, but it started with the leadership. Furthermore, the attitude of respect had to extend to the other people who supported the company. He couldn't cheat his suppliers while expecting his employees to operate with integrity. To keep employees and customers engaged, he had to lead by example, and he had to create an organization where everyone had the opportunity to participate, make a difference, see the results, and be celebrated.

Conclusion

*Not everything that can be counted counts, and
not everything that counts can be counted.*
—Albert Einstein

*The single most important thing to remember about
any enterprise is that there are no results inside its
walls. The result of a business is a satisfied customer.*
—Peter Drucker

*In the future, the companies with tremendous
relationship capital will be the ones that succeed.*
—Gary Vaynerchuk

*Individual commitment to a group effort.
That is what makes a team work, a company
work, a society work, a civilization work.*
—Vince Lombardi

*A society grows great when old men plant trees
whose shade they know they shall never sit in.*
—Greek Proverb

Introduction

"Times have changed since you started here," the CEO told Patrick. "Are you sure you're ready for this job?"

The two of them reflected on all that they had been through together. Sometimes it exhausted them trying to keep up with all of the changes. Technology and communication channels constantly changed. Their workforce spanned more generations, with a broader range of expectations, than ever before. Their footprints had been spread over a larger area, with an increasingly large array of products and services offered. Many jobs once done by humans were now done by machines, and they were just about to move forward with acquiring a company only slightly smaller than theirs.

As they reflected, something dawned on the CEO. "Nothing has really changed at all, has it? LUCK works now like it worked a thousand years ago. We're just developing more ways to scale it to work with larger groups of people," she observed.

The conversation took place during Patrick's last meeting with the outgoing CEO before heading back to the North Carolina coast to celebrate St. Patrick's Day with his family. When he returned to the office, it would be as the new CEO of the company.

She wished Patrick success once more, shook his hand, and said good-bye.

In The Lion's Den

"Surprise!"

People popped out from behind the bar, tables, and sofas as Patrick walked into The Lion's Den that Saturday morning of the St. Patrick's Day parade. The banner hung across the middle of the store read, "Congratulations, New CEO!!!"

Many of the people who had taught Patrick so much about relationships were there to show their support: People who had worked in The Lion's Den many years before ... Some of the businesspeople who had generously donated their time during Patrick's field trips ... A few of the businesspeople that Patrick had helped with their own LUCK ... Ann, who was now the majority owner of the Vines to Wines store next door, and part owner of a nearby vineyard and winery ... Jimmy, the leader of the motorcycle ride that visited every year—Patrick had joined Jimmy on the annual Carolina Coastal Cruise eight years ago and hadn't missed a ride since then ... Bert, the author, and Judy, his wife—four years ago one of Bert's books had become a bestseller, and he sold the movie rights on condition they filmed portions at The Lion's Den, and as a result, they had expanded to three stores along the coast and their own brand of roasted coffee ... Larry was there too; his business was now on solid ground ... Many of the co-owners of the many businesses and additional coffee shops Lauren now owned were also there ... And of course, his mother and his Aunt Mal were there too.

Patrick felt a lump in his throat. "I should be celebrating all of these people," he thought. "These are the giant shoulders I'm standing on!"

He felt a hand on his arm. "I'm so glad I could be here to thank you and celebrate with you." Patrick turned and was shocked to be looking at the CEO who had been the leader of his company for so many years and was now retiring. She never made a habit of making appearances at these types of events.

Patrick made his way around the room, thanking everyone and visiting with old friends and acquaintances. As each person hugged him and congratulated him, they handed him a small card. The same "Good LUCK" card his friend had handed him a few moments before he walked into The Lion's Den, and Patrick realized these cards had been printed for this celebration—not for St. Patrick's Day after all.

"I'd like to propose a toast to Patrick," said the retiring CEO. Another surprise. In spite of her tenacity and drive as CEO, she shied away from the limelight. Patrick had never heard her speak in public before.

"I've learned so much from watching you, Patrick," she began. "Maybe even a few things you didn't even realize yourself, so let me share a few of those things. I've learned that the people you taught to practice LUCK individually were the first and fastest to embrace it in business—it's important that people embrace LUCK if they expect a business to embrace LUCK. And you always talk about it not being all about technology, and that's true, but I've also learned we could have never scaled it the way we did without technology. I've learned that LUCK isn't just isolated to a few things, but it works for everything—for meetings, projects, planning, sales, and marketing. It applies to everything related to people. You, Patrick, followed the LUCK process for getting our organization to embrace LUCK! And it's important that we apply it to ourselves, which is what I have been doing in thinking through my retirement and what I will do with the second half of my life.

"And, in part because of you," she concluded, "I'm able to retire much sooner than I had ever imagined. I hope you have the same Good LUCK as CEO that I have enjoyed! Here's to you, Patrick!"

"Here, here," answered everyone in The Lion's Den as they raised their glasses.

"And now your mother, Aunt Mal, and I have a little gift for you," she continued. "That journal of yours has inspired too many people for you to continue to keep it to yourself. So we want you to have this." She handed Patrick a tablet computer in a leather cover with the words "Good LUCK" engraved on the front. "With this journal, you can collaborate and share knowledge with others inside and outside of the company, so more people can participate in developing LUCK and in benefiting from LUCK. It's a LUCK journal...scaled!"

Patrick beamed. This gift symbolized everything he had set out to do all those years ago. He had considered replacing his journal with a computer, but he could never give up the sentimental value attached to the original journal his mother had given him all those years ago. Now, with a tablet that included a cover made by Lauren, Patrick would retire his old worn journal and switch to this new one.

Later, as the party began to die down, the CEO asked Patrick if he would sit and speak with her for a few minutes. They sat in the large easy chairs by the front window of the shop.

"Patrick," she began, "I meant what I said about retirement. I'm retiring with a lot of life ahead of me, and I owe some credit to you for that. When you first talked with me about LUCK, I thought that it would be a one-time project and—when you were done—you would move on to other things. But it has become clear to me that LUCK is a process that never stops making us a better company for our customers and for our people. We've been around the circle of L-U-C-K many times and do it better with each successive pass. Our processes improve, our technology improves, and the ability of our people to deliver on LUCK improves—and we grow."

She spoke more about the role of LUCK in the changing the world, how relationships were the only assets that businesses and people really had—and how much truer that would become as automation, robotics, and other technologies continued to overtake traditional jobs. "The role of people for the next hundred years will increasingly focus on innovation, creativity, and engaging with other people, and LUCK is the framework for them to understand that.

"Which has given me inspiration for what to do with the second half of my life," she continued. "You know I would never be happy playing golf for the rest of my life. But I need your permission for what I want to do. I want to start a consulting firm that helps businesses find the same success we have found through The LUCK Principle. This is your baby, and I won't do it without your blessing, and I also don't want to do it without you. I'd like your permission to start this organization, and I'd like you to consider taking the position of chairman of our board of directors."

"That is a thrill to hear," Patrick responded after allowing a few moments for her proposal to sink in. "You need to know that the fertile ground you provided where LUCK could grow is rare. Now that I've been working with other companies to help them apply LUCK, I find everyone wants to transform their businesses—to go from aging country roads full of potholes to superhighways—but few have realistic expectations. Some expect to just pave enough potholes to create a superhighway. Others forget that building a relationship infrastructure is like building any other infrastructure; there is ongoing incremental construction as new roads are built and others are widened. Expect some frustration as you help others to understand this.

"Of course I'd be glad to be on your board and see you spread LUCK to others," Patrick concluded. As the years went by, Patrick would champion the creation of a branch of the business to aid nonprofit organizations and businesses in developing countries. His goal was to apply The LUCK Principle to accelerate their success and the success of their customers, volunteers, donors, and employees. By the time he retired, they had branched into providing training on The LUCK Principle to individuals who wanted to apply the principles of good relationships to every part of their lives.

The party died down, and the guests said their farewells to Patrick and began filtering out. Before Patrick knew it, his week at home had ended, and Sunday morning arrived. His mother and Aunt Mal sat with him at breakfast that morning before he left for the airport.

"Well, Mr. Business Executive," said Aunt Mal as she gave him a hug, "I guess this is good-bye for a while."

Then he turned toward Lauren. She grabbed him by both of his shoulders and held him at arm's length, looking him in the eye. "What's next for my Patrick?" she said, glowing with pride. "You always surprise me, but there's one thing I know you'll take wherever you go."

As she hugged him good-bye, she said, "Good LUCK, baby... Good LUCK."

Journal Entry

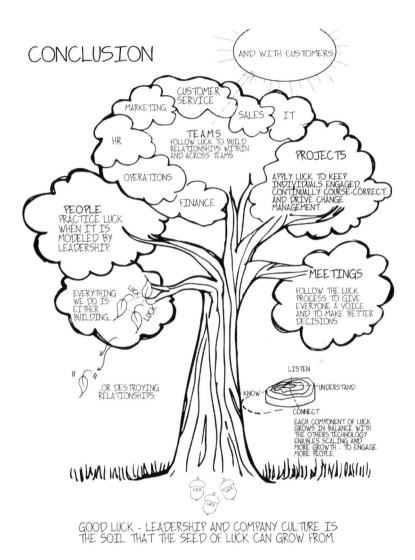

CONCLUSION

AND WITH CUSTOMERS

CUSTOMER SERVICE

MARKETING

SALES   IT

TEAMS
FOLLOW LUCK TO BUILD
RELATIONSHIPS WITHIN
AND ACROSS TEAMS.

HR

PROJECTS

APPLY LUCK TO KEEP
INDIVIDUALS ENGAGED,
CONTINUALLY COURSE-CORRECT
AND DRIVE CHANGE
MANAGEMENT.

OPERATIONS

FINANCE

PEOPLE
PRACTICE LUCK
WHEN IT IS
MODELED BY
LEADERSHIP.

MEETINGS

FOLLOW THE LUCK
PROCESS TO GIVE
EVERYONE A VOICE
AND TO MAKE BETTER
DECISIONS.

EVERYTHING
WE DO IS
EITHER
BUILDING...

LUCK
LUCK

LISTEN

KNOW   UNDERSTAND

...OR DESTROYING
RELATIONSHIPS.

CONNECT

EACH COMPONENT OF LUCK
GROWS IN BALANCE WITH
THE OTHERS. TECHNOLOGY
ENABLES SCALING AND
MORE GROWTH - TO ENGAGE
MORE PEOPLE.

LUCK
LUCK

GOOD LUCK - LEADERSHIP AND COMPANY CULTURE IS
THE SOIL THAT THE SEED OF LUCK CAN GROW FROM.

DIVE DEEPER

Next Steps

Squeezing a concept as broad as LUCK into a small book means I could only scratch the surface. Successfully applying the concepts found in the book can take many years and a great deal of additional knowledge beyond what can be found within this book. Use the resources in this section to deepen your knowledge and to continue to inspire your team along the path to making your own LUCK.

LUCK Resources

The website has all sorts of resources to help you put LUCK into practice. And I'll continually expand it with new resources. Subscribe to the LUCK blog and download the latest LUCK updates and resources, including more detailed versions of info-graphics and case studies in LUCK, by visiting the website:

www.theLUCKprinciple.com

Connect

This book is all about engagement. So, of course, I want to engage with you!

I would be honored for you to review the book on the website of your favorite bookseller, and I would love to hear from you on social media, or email. I'll respond to every single one! You can reach me @C5geoff on Twitter, or geoff@c5insight.com.

Join the Movement, Win Some Swag!

Have some fun, connect with others, help to create more people-centric workplaces, and win some sweet Lion's Den merchandise!

Submit a photo of you, The LUCK Principle book, and a social post with a favorite quote via Twitter, Facebook or Instagram. The quote can be from The LUCK Principle or another source of your choosing.

Each week I'll choose a winning photo and one LUCKY winner will receive their choice of a cozy *Lion's Den Coffee Company hoodie*, or a handmade *Lion's Den Coffee Mug with travel lid*!

But wait … there's more! After 1 year, I'll select a group of finalists for a vote. The winner will receive a $250.00 Amazon gift card.

Visit www.theLUCKprinciple.com to learn more and sign up.

Bring LUCK to Your Company or Event

My team at C5 Insight and I provide advisory services, planning, training workshops, talks, audits, analysis, implementation, bulk book specials, and inspiring keynote speeches for companies and organizations around the globe. We can help you improve how you engage with your customers and employees. Visit www.C5insight.com for details.

Dive Deeper

The books listed below, and other resources available on the web from the authors, provide a tremendous breadth and depth of additional information on many of the concepts found in *The LUCK Principle*. I highly recommend each and every one of them.

Brown, Dr. Brené. *Daring Greatly.* New York, NY: Avery, 2012.

Collins, Jim. *Good to Great.* USA: Harper Publishing, 2001.

Covey, Stephen. *The 7 Habits of Highly Effective People.* New York, NY: Simon & Schuster, 2013.

Covey, Sean & McChesney, Chris & Huling, Jim. *The 4 Disciplines of Execution.* New York, NY: Free Press, April, 2012.

Dixon, Matthew & Adamson, Brent. *The Challenger Sale.* New York, NY: Portfolio, 2011.

Grant, Adam. *Give and Take.* New York, NY: Penguin, 2013.

Johnson, Spencer & Blanchard, Kenneth. *Who Moved My Cheese?* New York, NY: Penguin Putnam Inc., 1998.

Li, Charlene. *The Engaged Leader: A Strategy for Your Digital Transformation.* Philadelphia, PA: Wharton Digital Press, 2015.

Manning, Harley & Bodine, Kerry. *Outside In.* New York, NY: Forrester & Amazon, 2012.

Meister, Jeanne C. & Willyerd, Karie. *The 2020 Workplace: How Innovative Companies Attract, Develop and Keep Tomorrow's Employees Today.* New York, NY: HarperBusiness, 2010.

Smart, Roland. *The Agile Marketer.* Hoboken, NJ: John Wiley & Sons, Inc., 2016.

Stack, Jack & Burlingham, Bo. *The Great Game of Business.* New York, NY: Crown Business, 2013.

END NOTES

The content in this book, and much of the inspiration for it, comes from client experiences, research, in-person interviews, and other books. Infographic data sources are specifically referenced below.

Some web addresses may be changed or content may be removed. Web content cited was available at the time the book was written.

Introduction

[1] Gallup, *State of the American Workplace*, (2013), http://employeeengagement.com/wp-content/uploads/2013/06/Gallup-2013-State-of-the-American-Workplace-Report.pdf

[2] Nucleus Research, "CRM Pays Back $8.71 for Every Dollar Spent," (2014), http://nucleusresearch.com/research/single/crm-pays-back-8-71-for-every-dollar-spent/

[3] C5 Insight, *CPR for CRM Study*, (2014) https://www.c5insight.com/Resources/CPRforCRM/tabid/111/Default.aspx; AIIM, *Connecting and Optimizing SharePoint*, (2015), http://info.aiim.org/connecting-and-optimizing-sharepoint

Chapter 1: Listen

[1] Zendesk, *Omnichannel Customer Service Gap Survey*, (2013), https://www.zendesk.com/resources/omnichannel-customer-service-report/

[2] Accenture, *Big Success with Big Data*, (2014), https://www.accenture.com/us-en/insight-big-data-research

[3] The CMO Club and Rakuten Marketing, *The CMO Solution Guide: Demystifying Omnichannel Marketing to Create a Winning Strategy for CMO's*, 2015, http://blog.marketing.rakuten.com/omni-report

[4] SmartFocus, *Marketing Pain Points and How to Overcome Them*, (2015), https://econsultancy.com/reports/marketing-pain-points-and-how-to-overcome-them/; "The New Science of Sales Performance," Harvard Business Review, (2014) https://hbr.org/resources/pdfs/comm/anaplan/anaplan_may_report_final.pdf

[5] C5 Insight, *CPR for CRM Study*, (2014) https://www.c5insight.com/Resources/CPRforCRM/tabid/111/Default.aspx

Chapter 2: Understand

[1] IBM, *Leading through Connections: Insights from the IBM Global CEO Study*, (2012), http://www-935.ibm.com/services/us/en/c-suite/ceostudy2012/

[2] EMC, *The Digital Universe of Opportunities: Rich Data and the Increasing Value of the Internet of Things*, (2014), https://www.emc.com/collateral/analyst-reports/idc-digital-universe-2014.pdf

[3] AIIM, Automating Information Governance, (2014), http://www.aiim.org/Resources/Research/Industry-Watches/2014/2014_May_InfoGov

[4] Brodkin, Jon, "You Are Wasting Time. Find Out Why. The Cost of Ineffective Search," NetworkWorld, (2007) http://www.network-

world.com/article/2303260/software/you-are-wasting-time--find-out-why.html

[5] Smith, Mark, Ventana Research, *The Mandate for Social Collaboration in Business*, (2012), https://marksmith.ventanaresearch.com/2012/06/28/the-mandate-for-social-collaboration-in-business/

[6] Aberdeen Group, *Executive Dashboards: The Key to Unlocking Double Digit Profit Growth*, (2009), http://www.bizreport.com/whitepapers/executive_dashboards_the_key_to.html

[7] Nucleus Research, *Business Analytics Pays Back $13.01 for Every Dollar Spent*, (2014), http://nucleusresearch.com/research/single/analytics-pays-back-13-01-for-every-dollar-spent/

Chapter 3: Connect

[1] Aral, Sinan; Brynjolfsson, Erik; Van Alstyne, Marshall, "Information, Technology and Information Worker Productivity," MIT, (2011), http://ebusiness.mit.edu/research/papers/2011.09_Aral_Brynjolfsson_Van%20Alstyne_Information%20Technology%20and%20Information%20Worker%20Productivity_277.pdf

[2] Kauderer, Steven; O'Neill, Sean; Whelan, David, "Why it Pays for P&C Insurers to Earn Their Customers Intense Loyalty," Bain Brief, (2013), http://www.bain.com/publications/articles/why-it-pays-for-pc-insurers-to-earn-their-customers-intense-loyalty-brief.aspx

[3] Corner Stone OnDemand, *Toxic Employees in the Workplace*, (2015), https://www.cornerstoneondemand.com/sites/default/files/thank-you/file-to-download/csod-wp-toxic-employees-032015_0.pdf

[4] The Sales Management Association, *Research Update: Sales Process Adoption and Usage*, (2013), http://salesmanagement.org/events/single-article/research-update-sales-process-adoption-and-usage

[5] Cross, Rob; Gray, Peter; Cunningham, Shirley; Shower, Mark; Thomas, Robert J., "The Collaborative Organization: How to Make Employee Networks Really Work," The MIT Sloan Review, (2010), http://sloanreview.mit.edu/article/the-collaborative-organization-how-to-make-employee-networks-really-work/

Chapter 4: Know

[1] Aberdeen Group, *Executive Dashboards: The Key to Unlocking Double Digit Profit Growth*, (2009), http://www.bizreport.com/whitepapers/executive_dashboards_the_key_to.html

[2] The Social Workplace, *Social Knows: Employee Engagement Statistics*, (2011), http://www.thesocialworkplace.com/2011/08/social-knows-employee-engagement-statistics-august-2011-edition/

[3] Yip, Jeffrey; Ernst, Chris; Campbell, Michael, "Boundary Spanning Leadership," (2011), http://insights.ccl.org/wp-content/uploads/2015/04/BoundarySpanningLeadership.pdf

Chapter 5: Good LUCK

[1] Keil, Fred, *Return on Character*, (2015), https://www.amazon.com/Return-Character-Reason-Leaders-Companies/dp/1625271301

[2] Heskett, James, *The Culture Cycle: How to Shape the Unseen Force that Transforms Performance*, (2012), https://www.amazon.

com/Culture-Cycle-Transforms-Performance-Paperback/
dp/0134387074/ref=sr_1_1?s=books&ie=UTF8&qid=146861284
7&sr=1-1&keywords=the+culture+cycle

[3] "Americans Still Lack Trust in Company Management Post-Recession," BusinessWire, (2011), http://www.businesswire.com/news/home/20110711005277/en/Americans-Lack-Trust-Company-Management-Post-Recession

[4] Modern Survey, Webinar, (undated), https://attendee.gotowebinar.com/recording/340888559056374274

43166943R00085

Made in the USA
Middletown, DE
02 May 2017